About the Author

Frank Wingate lived in Hong Kong from 1978 to 2000, witnessing the vast economic and social changes that engulfed China and metamorphosed the territory, as well as the final return to Chinese sovereignty. Arriving as a teacher, he became a freelance journalist and public relations executive in turn, before founding his own business. He now lives in Kingston, UK.

Dedication

To my wife Uschi, and my children Florian and Sophie.

Frank Wingate

POXY CHICKEN:

SWEET AND SOUR MEMORIES
OF
HONG KONG'S LAST
COLONIAL YEARS

AUSTIN MACAULEY
PUBLISHERS LTD.

A CIP catalogue record for this title is available from the British Library.

ISBN 978 1 78455 765 2 (Paperback)
ISBN 978 1 78455 767 6 (Hardback)

www.austinmacauley.com

First Published (2015)
Austin Macauley Publishers Ltd.
25 Canada Square
Canary Wharf
London
E14 5LB

Printed and bound in Great Britain

Contents

Poxy Chicken

When I arrived in Hong Kong, at the start of a great adventure, in December 1977, I already had a job lined up. St Paul's Boys School, one of Hong Kong's more prestigious English-medium schools, had offered me a temporary position, covering for a member of staff on maternity leave. Little did I think then, that my two-year planned dalliance with Hong Kong would turn into a 22-year-long love affair.

St Paul's had responded to one of several letters I had written from the UK, enquiring after teaching posts, both permanent and short term. After nearly four years' teaching in Yorkshire, my first position, I rated myself as qualified, having survived what seemed at the time like a rigorous apprenticeship.

As many new teachers did, I had approached my first job with an excess of self-confidence. I was sure I would instinctively connect with the pupils – speak their language – and fashion a progressive, personal and productive relationship with them. The coalminers' sons of Pontefract, however, were a gritty, no-nonsense, down-to-earth lot, with little interest in any namby-pamby approaches of an idealistic student teacher.

They ran rings round me for the first two years and made my life a misery. I would have packed it in altogether, were it not for the support and guidance of experienced and sympathetic colleagues, who assured me this was all part of a familiar learning process. One thing helped – that was my

9

sporting ability. As a games teacher and youthful member of the staff rugby team, I was able to show some sporting toughness which earned me a level of respect. I battered them on the field and my credibility rose. This was, after all, rugby league country.

Initially the boys at King's School regarded me as a southern softie. "Ee Sir, ye talk like a reet pufta," was a regular reaction to my southern vowels. Nevertheless, I gradually earned respect and control, and after three years considered myself, if not top of the profession, at least a passable practitioner.

But I was itching to move on. One reason I chose teaching as a career was because in those days of lingering British cultural influence around the world, it offered travel and overseas career opportunities. When the chance of an extended stay in Hong Kong arose, courtesy of the generous parents of my girlfriend at the time, I leapt at it. It wasn't the first international post I had applied for – the Head of History position at the Girl's Grammar School in Bermuda had led to a final interview, but for some unknown reason, I had not been selected. I like to think it was on account of my youthful good looks and potential threat to the maidens' virtue.

Finally then, when Dr Ha, the headmaster of St Paul's School in Hong Kong, replied with a job offer, fate pointed to the British colony. On arrival though, I still had almost two months to occupy myself, and money was tight, so my first teaching efforts were directed at private tuition. This was a relatively easy option, as the Hong Kong Chinese were keen to learn English and native speakers, far less qualified than me, were making a living out of "conversation classes".

Consequently, I placed my ad in the South China Morning Post and waited for the phone to ring. Enquiries came thick and fast and within two days I had a number of private students lined up. They gave me my first personal contact with

Hong Kong people and some insight into their lives, which were very different from the expatriate circles I had been limited to in the first few weeks.

One of my first students was an earnest young man called Jason Chan. Jason was a charming, serious, pimply young man of about 20. He worked full-time in some kind of factory admin job, but, like so many young Hong Kong Chinese, was resolutely keen to improve himself. Consequently, he studied most evenings and spent some of his hard earned money paying me.

His English wasn't bad at all, but he aimed to be fluent and so, twice a week over those early months of 1978 I met him, in his tiny rented room in Causeway Bay, to pore over grammar books and repeatedly practise drills. He struggled with the auxiliary verb "to do" and we spent many lessons practising such sentences as "He didn't want to, did he?" or "She doesn't like it, does she? No, she doesn't."

I was a History rather than an English teacher by training and my time with Jason made me starkly aware of the complexities of the English verb structure. I suffered with him as he endured the torture of the continuous present perfect and implied future. "I am going to the shop tomorrow" can't be future, he complained with justification.

Getting to know Jason gave me immense admiration for those like-minded Cantonese, who were determined autodidacts and great respecters of learning – something lost back home. It also gave me a lesson about Hong Kong's cramped living conditions. I usually taught Jason in the tiny single room he rented – no bigger than a box room. Just enough space for a bed and a narrow desk. We sat side by side on his bed, spreading our books on the desk lid.

After I started a school job I stayed on with Jason for a couple of months, but instead of charging him I exchanged an hour of English for an hour of Cantonese.

Another private student I picked up was Dorothy Pao. An ex-British Airways hostess of independent means, she lived with her younger sister in a relatively spacious flat in the "middle class" area of Tai Hang Road. I suspect she was supported by a reasonably wealthy family, or even a sugar daddy boyfriend, but we never spoke of this.

She always spoiled me with offers of tea, sweets and soup, and flirted quite openly with me, though I was more interested in earning my money than spoiling the professional relationship. As time went on she wore more alluring clothing and eventually was offering me brandy and whiskey and asking me to stay after my allocated hour. However, by that time I had begun a full-time post and had to end the arrangement. Dorothy spoke English quite fluently and I think the lessons were as much a pleasant diversion as a serious intellectual endeavour.

Mr So was a different proposition. He was a well-to-do, immaculately dressed businessman, housed in a beautifully furnished large flat. I remember the carved dark mahogany dining table where we sat, rather formally, for his lessons. He had very specific pronunciation concerns. He struggled with the "R" sound in particular. Like many Cantonese speakers he confounded it with "L", simply because the Cantonese equivalent sound lies somewhere between the two.

"Purse your lips", I would say, "as if you were kissing someone". "Relax your tongue and keep it away from the sides and roof of your mouth. "RRRR...Really, Right, Red, Road" we intoned repeatedly. After a month and eight lessons of this he cracked it and I never had a more satisfied or grateful student in my entire teaching career.

"Thank you, thank you, Mr Wingate. I've been calling my son Lobert all these years and now I can say Robert, RRRRRobert," he repeated proudly. He stuffed an extra hundred Hong Kong dollars into my hand and we parted in mutual admiration.

Soon it was time for me to start my full-time post at St Paul's Boys school. This was regarded as one of Hong Kong's leading Anglo-Chinese secondary schools, one at which English was the medium of learning, affording it a higher status than the equivalent Chinese language institutions.

Housed in a plain building quite near Hong Kong University at the Western end of Mid-Levels on Hong Kong Island, the school was functional – both physically and educationally. There were no luxuries, nor any facilities we considered normal in the UK. For example, there were no playing fields, hardly a playground; no art rooms, no assembly hall and no dining areas. There were just plain classrooms, with 40 or more desks in tightly packed and uniform rows.

However, this was more than compensated for by the attentive, invariably cheerful, diligent and courteous students. I had hardly had a challenging time in the UK, teaching in a reputable small town grammar school, but compared with the blunt-speaking cocky Pontefract boys, the Hong Kong students were like an angelic host.

The challenges, however, were different. While there was no rowdiness to suppress, there was excessive passivity and deference – how I struggled to get my classes to answer questions, never mind engage in debate!

I would throw out a question to the class. Silence followed, heads bowed to the desk. Then I would pick a name from the tabulated list pinned to my teacher's desk. Wong Yiu Ming? Extreme embarrassment would ensue. Wong Yiu Ming would climb, red-faced, to his feet. But before he could answer, at least six boys around him would ensure he gave the correct answer by whispering it to him quite audibly.

When we discussed an essay topic, with suggestions, ideas and English vocabulary put on the blackboard, the framework and phrases were feverishly copied into notebooks. Consequently, I would find myself later marking 40 exercise books with almost identical essays in them.

This behaviour did change as they got to know their new, strange teacher from the UK, who had a beard and long hair. Teaching them was a joy. Simple techniques, such as pinning up outstanding work on the classroom walls, were met with both surprise and pleasure. In general, you could say these Chinese students were easy to teach, in the sense they were very diligent, earnest and ambitious. Their commitment to education and its value in self-improvement, was cultural, reinforced by an immigrant community's aspiration for betterment. In addition, there was a long tradition of respect for teachers. On the other hand they tended to lack originality and creativity and it was difficult to elicit individual opinions.

Most of them had adopted English names, because their teachers at primary school had encouraged them to do so. The result was sometimes amusing to the native English speaker as they didn't understand the cultural context. Consequently, I came across a Rambo Wong, a Vanky Mok, a Hitler Siu and a Vosper Song. "Why Vosper?" I asked. "Oh, it's Italian for scooter" was the reply.

The boys had classroom habits which were strange to me. There was the continual request to go to the toilet, not to relieve themselves, but to spit. Obviously, they didn't want to swallow their saliva! Another thing I noticed was the unusual way they held their pens. This was a tight grip, holding the pen upright between index and middle finger. It looked uncomfortable, but was a technique suitable for Chinese calligraphy.

Fellow teachers were supportive and helpful. I was one of only three expat teachers there. One was an elusive, quietly mysterious American, who acted as Deputy Head to the kind but equally distant Dr Ha. He rarely appeared in public and, presumably, carried out mainly administrative duties. Apparently, he had been at the school for twenty years.

There was also Jim Barnes, another American, who weighed some 20 stone and seemed strangely out of place among the generally slender and graceful colleagues. Jim was very popular among the students, teaching English, and later went on to have a very successful one-man English private tuition business, from which he earned a great deal of money, but which saw him expand by another ten stone.

I never really became close with any Chinese colleagues. Whilst they were always supportive and kind, they regarded me as a temporary interloper and with my beard and Cat Stevens haircut, somewhat suspiciously. However, I got on famously with the students, who obviously considered it hugely entertaining to have this weird young, trendy teacher, who contrasted with their regular, very conservative, conventionally stern teachers.

Like all schoolboys they were mischievous and had their fun at my expense. For the first few weeks one class of 16-year-olds, who always stood on my entering the classroom, would greet me with a polite "Jo saan, lo su" which I reasonably understood to mean "Good morning, Sir." Only after a passing Chinese colleague overheard this and came in to scold the class in no uncertain terms, did it become clear that they were intoning "Good morning, rat", rather than "Jo saan, lo si", which would have been the correct greeting.

It was the boys at St Paul's who also christened me "Fat Wan Gai". This is a loose Cantonese syllabic equivalent to my name. It means "Poxy, or Dizzy Chicken", and somehow that nickname stuck with me throughout my Hong Kong years.

My time at St Paul's passed quickly. The maternity leave was concluded and Mrs Kwok returned to her role. After two months then I moved on to another "elite" English language school in Hong Kong – La Salle Boys' School. This came about because I was introduced to a La Salle teacher, Randy Woo Ho Wai, who was a friend of one of the St Paul's staff. Randy was a passionate History teacher and shared with me a love of his subject. He was dedicated, amusing, talkative and great fun. We hit it off immediately, discussing anything from Gladstone to Deng Xiaoping. We became colleagues and drinking friends, sharing our lives and families and the relationship became lifelong.

Woo alerted me to another temporary position at the distinguished La Salle Boys College, which had stringent entrance conditions and enjoyed high status in Hong Kong's education system. The school provided the upper echelons of Hong Kong's government and professional elites with a steady stream of talent. It was a sort of Eton or Harrow in that respect.

My job interview with the Headmaster was bizarre. La Salle College was still run by the Catholic teaching order of that name, but I didn't expect to be greeted by a monk in a classic monk's flowing white habit. But to my further surprise he was Irish. Father O'Brien was slightly taken aback by my "Cat Stevens" look of full, dark locks and beard, but he was patronisingly polite.

"And are you a Catholic, Mr Wingate?" he ventured. "No", I replied, guessing already that I had little chance of getting this job. "So I suppose you're Church of England, then?" "In theory, but actually I'm an atheist," I responded with all the cocksureness of my generation. "Oh, Bejasus," said Father O'Brien, "He's a heathen!"

As it turned out though, Father O'Brien wasn't going to let a little theological complexity get in the way of hiring a qualified native language teacher, and conveniently solving his temporary staff problem.

I was hired to teach English for six weeks. Father O'Brien raised a final complication before I left the room. "Mr Wingate, we'll be needing you in this post to teach lessons on the Catholic Catechism. Will that be agreeable?" This was difficult, but as I hesitated to consider my answer he demonstrated more holy pragmatism.

"Ah, don't worry, Mr Wingate, just teach it as a reading lesson!" And so I did.

La Salle students were probably even more studious than the St Paul's boys. They were taught in equally conservative style. Much reminded me of education in the UK in the 1950s. Formal and didactic, it typified the educational theory of filling the pitcher of water – i.e. filling the passive student with knowledge – as opposed to nurturing the plant, or encouraging individual organic development. Nevertheless, the school was not disciplinarian and the monks and staff teachers were considerate and sympathetic to the boys.

The College building itself was decrepit. It had a damp, musty smell and feel to it and even had mouldy patches on the walls in certain parts. Being in Kowloon, quite near Kai Tak airport, it was also very noisy, with planes swooping low over the school on their way to the runway.

In the over 30 degree summer heat and high humidity of Hong Kong, and without the luxury of air-conditioning, windows had to be flung open to cool the classrooms. This meant that every ten minutes, with the next jet roaring overhead at a little more than skyscraper height, our lesson had to be suspended until it had passed. We also had to hold on to ours pens and rulers, which would otherwise have been shaken to the floor from the desks.

Once again I was struck by the contrast of these ambitious students with the indifference or even hostility of many pupils in the UK to learning. Even in an "elite" school like La Salle, conditions were rudimentary, but this deterred none of them.

Teaching at La Salle, as at St Paul's, while not exhausting in terms of expenditure of nervous energy in the classroom, was tiring owing to the sheer volume of preparation and marking. Looking after a full schedule of classes of forty or more students and teaching English language, which requires precise, detailed and regular marking, meant that my school rucksack resembled an SAS standard combat pack on most days.

The contrast with my third and permanent teaching post in Hong Kong couldn't have been greater.

Through a friend I had learnt that the German-Swiss school in Hong Kong was looking for a new History teacher. As well as offering the standard German curriculum and exam system, so that the children of German expats could easily re-assimilate into the German system on returning home, the school also had an English stream, providing Cambridge GSCEs and GCEs (O and A levels).

Only a few years old, the school had been the brainchild of an exceptional visionary German lady – Inge Buchholz – who had originally envisioned a totally bilingual school at which both languages were to be used in teaching. It was a bold idea, but it proved impractical and so two distinct streams had emerged.

As the school was funded by the German, Swiss and Austrian governments, it was obliged to accept all children who had one parent from those countries. These weren't great numbers and so, to make the school financially viable the English stream was fee-paying – and one of the most expensive in Hong Kong.

An immediately striking feature of the school was its stunning location in the Peak district of Hong Kong, high on the southern side of the Island's mountainous spine. Overlooking a spectacular southern view of the South China Sea, it was smothered in hot, humid sunshine in the summer and blanketed in a dense humid fog for much of the day in winter.

My job interview was unexpectedly political. Probably because of my "radical" appearance, the German businessmen who dominated the selection committee were concerned that my social democratic values would contaminate their children. I had to assure them I was concerned with developing the students' own views and not indoctrinating or brainwashing them.

My new students were widely diverse – in nationality and ability. In one aspect they were similar; they came from wealthy backgrounds. As a result the only problems we had as their teachers revolved around them being materially spoilt, but emotionally deprived. Some of the older students came to school driving their own quality brand sports cars; others were driven in Bentleys or BMWs by the family driver; some of them rarely saw their parents and were looked after by servants.

This all amounted to a luxury teaching environment. My largest classes were twenty students, so I could finally indulge myself with quality lesson preparation, rather than the drudgery of continuous marking. My GCE A level sets never had more than four students, so I could coach and individually tutor. Disciplinary problems were non-existent.

For three of the four years I taught at GSIS as we called it, I was form teacher of one set of students, taking them from form 2 (12 years old) to form 4. We had 20 nationalities in a class averaging 24 – British, American, Chinese, Indian, German, Dutch, Swedish, Danish, Filipino, Canadian, Japanese, Taiwanese, Australian, New Zealand, Singaporean, South African, Argentinian, Korean, Thai and Lebanese.

Logically, I taught this junior UN a world history course, with Chinese and Asian history featuring. They were a delightful crowd and it was heart-warming to see adolescents betraying no hint of racism or intolerance in their dealing with each other.

How they enjoyed, at the end of school on Friday, my joke of the week. This popular institution was shared with their parents, who often commented on the standard of particular jokes, when they met me. "Pretty good this week, Mr Wingate," they might reflect, or "Last Friday's joke wasn't up to your normal standard".

I had few problems with parents, though some were unrealistic in their expectations of their not so academic offspring. At least I never experienced the direct pressure of some parents on colleagues to alter their children's grades with a threat of complaining to the school that the teacher had been "too harsh" in his marking.

I did have several American parents take me to task over my teaching of the Vietnam War, which was of course raw and recent. My general interpretation that the USA lost the war and was forced to withdraw was challenged by some patriots, but not discourteously.

The experience of this school's community gave me an insight into the richest element of expatriate Hong Kong society. Many of these financiers and international traders lived a life of fabulous comfort with luxury houses and flats and teams of servants.

It was a strange dichotomy that amid this wealth I, like some other teachers, lived modestly on a local salary. Not that I complained. It supported a comfortable lifestyle, with 12 paid weeks holiday a year. In addition, the younger teachers, German and English, formed a lively social group, all of us relatively new to Hong Kong and Asia and keen to explore our new habitat.

Our group enjoyed frequent weekend socialising and partying with bouts of drinking, so we decided to formally create the Hong Kong Anglo-German Organisation for Virtuous Education and Recreation, or HANGOVER for short. We discovered hiking routes in the hinterland and on the islands of Hong Kong and experimented boldly with exotic Chinese food.

It seemed to me I had come a long way from being a student teacher in Yorkshire, not very competently learning my trade, to a privileged and relatively relaxed role, confident in a cosmopolitan environment, in faraway Hong Kong.

But after four years in this ivory tower I became restless again. Partly because I reached thirty years old and was still earning a small salary, which hardly allowed me to rent a flat in Hong Kong; and partly because I wanted to work in the real Hong Kong, not a detached expatriate fishbowl.

For these reasons I decided to resign and look for a new career, which was easier in Hong Kong than it might have been in London. I had enjoyed teaching, particularly in Hong Kong, but now looked to journalism and the media for new opportunities.

My days as a Hong Kong teacher came to an end, but not my days as an adventurer in Hong Kong. On the contrary, a new chapter was just beginning, and the experience of teaching had given me the confidence and skills to risk another career path. Hong Kong was just the environment for taking a risk.

The Golden Dragon

An invitation to a Hong Kong and Shanghai Bank party was rare and something to be valued, so Larry, my bachelor friend, and I, were quite excited to receive one. "The Bank", as it was grandly referred to, had an elite position in Hong Kong society, along with Jardine and Matheson and Swires, the two great trading houses which dominated the Hong Kong commercial world in the old days. Long before it became a leading global force, and reduced its name to the acronym HSBC, "The Bank" prospered on China trade and its privileged strategic position in the British colony.

It hired mostly Oxbridge graduates for its management training programmes and paid them well. These were the days when only a few of the very brightest Chinese had a chance of reaching any senior position. This was the golden era for bright young expats, who made it into the ranks of "The Bank". They rarely returned to the misty climes of home – but died rich, spoiled and happy in the Orient, content in the belief of their own British superiority and right to govern.

Neither Larry nor I seemed destined for this expatriate heaven. Larry was a junior government officer – reasonably paid, secure and provided with accommodation – but definitely not in the same league as Bank employees. As for me, I was a humble school teacher, who had ventured out to Hong Kong without expatriate contractual status. On a local salary, and renting my own small flat in a Chinese block, I was certainly at the lower end of the expat pecking order.

Being a competent soccer player, however, did help level the imbalance, for the sport followed the British, Scots, Irish and Germans around the colonial world. In the more democratic environs of the Hong Kong Football Club, I was in a relatively egalitarian social milieu. The fact I had a good left foot and a strong pair of lungs propelled me into the first team and a status which made up in large part for my lack of income and expatriate credentials.

This explains why Larry and I had received the Bank party invite. One of my team mates was, indeed, a successful young manager in waiting, and invited us along to the official Bank gathering. I suspect, looking back, that it was in an irresponsible moment of post-match bonhomie, when he was off-guard, for the two of us had something of a reputation for being "lively" party guests.

The reputation had been gained following a sophisticated invitation to another bastion of affluent self-indulgence – the Hong Kong Club. This elegant social club attracted the expatriate and Chinese business elites with its lavish surroundings and impeccable service. Larry and I had been recommended as suitable escorts to two young ladies – twins – whose father wanted a couple of presentable and good-looking lads to accompany his daughters to the Hong Kong Club New Year's Dinner. Presentable and good-looking we were – but probably not suitable.

We scrubbed up well. I invested in a black, velvet corduroy jacket to stand in for the dinner jacket I didn't own, and borrowed a bow tie. To cut a long story short, the evening went quite well until after midnight. Then serious deterioration set in as the quantities of champagne, beer and white wine took their toll. The twins were courteous, but aloof and dull as ditchwater. Their mother and father were much more fun.

Unfortunately, the girls' elder sister offended Larry about something or other during a slurred argument. It resulted in an irritated Larry thumping the table firmly to make a point. Regrettably, he failed to notice the dish of blancmange that had been placed at the very point of impact.

After further confusion, dispute, allegations and denials, as well as considerable wiping down of faces and clothing with napkins, we were asked to leave, and this was the cause of our "reputation" as rabble-rousers. Nevertheless, we determined to outgrow this unfair slur and prove ourselves worthy of sophisticated and polite company. The Bank invite was very welcome in this respect. We needed to prove that we were worthy participants in social intercourse at the summit of Hong Kong society.

I don't remember now what the occasion for the Bank party was. It may have been a welcome for a batch of newcomers to the Bank managerial training scheme. Strangely though, it was set in a Bank building in Mongkok. This was unusual, because Mongkok was a thoroughly Chinese part of mainland Hong Kong. It was recorded in the Guinness Book of Records as the most densely populated area in the world.

With soaring high rises of dubious construction quality, teeming tenements, narrow streets and alleys, full of shops, hawkers, stalls, barrows, markets and people, Mongkok was both fascinating and a little scary for the average expat. The planes heading for Kai Tak airport deliberately flew fifty feet over the rooftops – or so it seemed.

Few people there spoke English. It was supposedly a den for triad gangsters. Criminals hid in dark shadows from the Hong Kong police and decent young expat males did not venture there after dark. At least, not off the beaten track.

The other strange feature of the party was that it required fancy dress. This wasn't particularly unexpected for the expat community had a weird obsession with dressing up, from the Governor, in his splendid ostrich feather hat, down to modern day party-goers, who kitted up in bizarre costumes for their

Saturday night out. It was strange for Larry and me, however, who didn't take easily to ostentation and exhibitionism.

Some relief was afforded by the topic of fancy dress, however. The "1960s" theme seemed within reach and not too outlandish. I would have baulked at being a pirate, a mummy or a samurai, but a 1960s hippy? No problem – why, I even had some of the fashion of the 60s in my current wardrobe.

I dug out my old, battered, bell-bottomed jeans – the white ones. I found my paisley shirt with the extra-long collar. This basic uniform was then adorned with various bead necklaces and amulets that I could scrape together. The tour de force, however, was a long black haired wig, in the style of Frank Zappa in his prime.

I tied this up with a bandanna and topped off the whole ridiculous garb with some John Lennon type round, small-lens sunglasses. On the day of the Bank party, I assembled this wardrobe, which would not have looked out of place at Woodstock or a Jimmy Hendrix concert, but was bizarre for late 1970s Hong Kong, and set forth into a steamy Hong Kong evening.

The first leg of my journey was to head over Hong Kong harbour to meet up with Larry at his small flat in an area called Hung Hom. This I achieved by using the Star Ferry. In my hippy garb I attracted many stares and comments, but everyone was too polite or shy to say anything directly to me.

Hong Kong people were quite aware of the peace and love and rock music revolution, but the youngsters were on the whole very conventional. Hong Kong teenagers in those days were much more concerned with education and career progress, having had the virtues of hard work and material security drummed into them by their parents. In the majority of cases they had fled to Hong Kong as refugees with barely the clothes they stood in.

When I reached Larry's there was a good deal of mutual hilarity. He too had risen to the occasion with purple shirt, bell-bottoms, wig, sheepskin coat (utterly impractical in the humidity and heat) and a fedora hat. And so we set off for the Bank location in Mongkok, looking like a couple of part-time actors who had wandered off a film set and got themselves lost.

We did get lost too in the narrow, crowded streets of Mongkok, which, eight-o-clock in the evening, were bustling with packed crowds of shoppers, diners, families window shopping, shouts and traffic noise. No-one even noticed a couple of weirdly dressed expats in this cacophony of noise and colour. Having emerged from the Mongkok stop of the Hong Kong underground, Larry and I spent the next hour trying the find the Bank building. We were new to this particular area and the map on the invite was illegible and inaccurate.

As a result of our directionless wanderings around this area, we finally turned up a little late, somewhat stressed and certainly very hot and uncomfortable, particularly Larry in his sheepskin coat. He was perspiring heavily and his blonde wig was visibly wilting.

The Bank's headquarters in Mongkok was a dark, grey-granite building – solid, imposing and safe -- as you would expect a bank to be. It was fashioned after a kind of blockhouse, being devoid of any architectural merit.

When we finally entered the room of the party, which was obviously a large cocktail-style affair with at least a hundred people attending, we were given a shock. Far from melting effortlessly into a heaving hippy celebration, we found ourselves facing an elegant crowd of young, sophisticated executives, not one of whom has obviously interpreted the party invitation fashion call in the way Larry and I had. We stuck out like sore thumbs. Too late now, however. We had no choice but to brazen it out, and that's exactly what we did.

Some people gawped, pointed at us and nudged each other. But most were too busy partying anyway, and the lights weren't too bright. Our football mate host, who had invited us, explained that everyone was in 1960s fashion but that was "smart" fashion. I did detect a couple of mods and even a rocker too, but they didn't really look like the real thing.

The whole affair could have become an embarrassment of major proportions. We could have baled out, made early excuses and left. However, there was very decent champagne to be had, served by straight-faced Chinese waiters (very few of the guests were Chinese), who for some reason failed to respond to the general bonhomie Larry and I imparted when reaching for yet another glass.

They obviously disapproved of hippies, and probably detected from our gauche behaviour that we were not authentic "Bank" staff.

As the champagne dissolved the feelings of awkwardness and stiffened the self-confidence, we made valiant attempts to mingle with the other guests. These efforts were not entirely fruitless. I do remember having a spirited argument about banking's role in the capitalist system and putting a crude Marxist spin on the theme. This line of discussion seemed to leave those in the conversation with the view that I was stark, staring mad. They made their excuses and courteously slipped away.

Naturally, like all red-blooded young men, we made energetic efforts to engage with some of the fashionable young ladies there. As we clearly couldn't rely on style and appearance, we turned to flattery and humour to approach them. This had limited success too. Most of them seemed to be called Lucinda, Penelope, or Stephanie.

Not that people were unfriendly or impolite, but we were clearly regarded as harmless freaks who had probably crashed the party. Once it was obvious we were not part of the greater Bank family, interest in us evaporated. So the evening wore on, in an increasing haze of champagne-induced wellbeing. The quality of social intercourse deteriorated, though we made lifelong friends with a number of other equally well-oiled outcasts by the end.

The end came at about two o'clock in the morning, when we were politely ushered out by the patient staff into the still sticky, breathless air of a Hong Kong night. We were, by that time, slightly unsteady on our feet, but considerably pleased that we had acquitted ourselves so successfully at such a chic party – so we thought.

Before us was the challenge of finding our way back to the underground station. We had managed to lose ourselves within four hundred yards on the way here, and that was sober. Small wonder we were soon teetering through entirely unknown Mongkok backstreets. Like most of Hong Kong, the streets were still fully lit late at night, with neon signs ablaze, and a good number of people still went about their mysterious ways.

Had we been sober, however, we might have been a good deal more cautious. There was some truth in Mongkok's unsalutory reputation, because the police did find it hard to track fugitives down in Mongkok's warrens of tower blocks and alleys. It was easy to remain anonymous, and, traditionally, Hong Kong working folk did not particularly trust the police. A kind of Mafia omerta, or community silence, underpinned by triad threats, meant that information was hard to come by.

These reflections didn't deter two inebriated hippies that night, however, from marching forth. Indeed, the overconfidence we had generated at the party led us to take a further risk. In one narrow alley, we saw the sign – "The

Golden Dragon". It was evidently a Chinese night club and one with a dubious offering.

We both knew this with some certainty, because the signage of Hong Kong nightclubs was recognisable, on account of the red-light neon and pictures of young ladies portrayed outside.

We had been to many Hong Kong nightclubs of varying moral standards, but there was an unwritten distinction between expat nightclubs, where anyone was welcome, and Chinese nightclubs, which would turn away expats. This was a rule we would normally have observed, but not that night.

We stumbled up the stairs, past the domestic altar, with its incense and paper money, and peered through the door. It was dark and smoky, with a central small bar, gloomily lit and two rows of cubicle like seating along the walls. We were being curious, and looking for a cold beer, but expected to be shown the door, particularly with our peculiar costumes and wigs.

"What do you want?" said an unfriendly voice, as the "Mama San" or manageress, came towards us.

"Oh, any chance of a beer?" I answered.

"Sit down, over there," she commanded brusquely, pointing to one of the cubicles.

As our eyes became accustomed to the gloom we began to unravel the scene. It was a small place – less than 1,000 square feet, with about eight cubicles, which could hold six people each. There weren't more than two or three other customers there, but we could make out the bar girls, or hostesses, in the shadows.

The Mama San gave us our beers. "You been party… eh?" she asked with a flicker of friendliness, smiling at our looks. We told her we had.

"You like buy pretty girls a drink?" she followed. Why not, we thought. Might meet someone interesting, someone exotic.

She called over two young women, who joined us and sat down. They were called Mimi and Lulu, or something very similar. They were young and attractive, and heavily made up. They spoke English quite well, enough to stimulate our interest; enough to flatter us. They were chatty and cheerful. After a while, the Mama San reappeared and suggested another round of drinks, which was an excellent and thoughtful idea. Our doubts about Chinese nightclubs were clearly unfounded. Here we were, us pioneers of night life, us brave explorers of oriental cultures, having a really good time. More drinks followed.

The good time lasted over an hour. But then the Mama San abruptly informed us that the club was closing. Our girls disappeared in a flash, hastily leaving without finishing their drinks or giving us their phone numbers. When the bill arrived, we instantly recognised why. It was over a thousand Hong Kong dollars. We had a problem.

At that point I took off my wig, to demonstrate my seriousness. So did Larry. I sobered up instantly. So did Larry. We looked at each other. Being braver than me he attempted to challenge the bill.

"Er…excuse me, there seems to be a mistake," he sallied feebly. "How much is a beer here?"

"No mistake," replied Mama San, with a harsh tone. "One beer, three dollars. Girl drink one hundred dollars. Girl company one hundred dollars one hour. You pay!" she added with a firm tone.

Now our choices were narrowing rapidly. Given these extortionate prices, the bill was correct. One option was to pay. We checked our finances. Together we could only muster forty-seven dollars. We could not pay. We could run for it. That was another option, until we noticed several men nearby.

Four of them came over with the Mama San. They didn't speak English, but the threatening tone of their Cantonese didn't need a professional interpreter. We had had our drinks and the girls' drinks and company and we weren't going anywhere until we paid. It was menacing and we feared we would face violence.

All we could do was bargain with the Mama San. We offered her all the money we had. We offered her our watches (mine was worth about 20 dollars!). And we offered IOUs. We pleaded rather pathetically for their understanding. We were sorry. We really didn't understand the way things worked in a Chinese night club. We didn't realise we had to pay for the girls' company. This went on for 15 minutes, until the men gradually lost interest and drifted off. It was clear we just couldn't pay. We wrote an IOU for the sum and I put my phone number on it.

I deliberately misspelt my name and put two false digits to my phone number. I didn't fancy the idea of Triads coming looking for me! They of course put no value on it at all, except to pressure us at the time.

Eventually, we bluffed ourselves out of an unpleasant situation. Still arguing with the Mama San, we sidled towards the door, and with many a false apology and penitent pleading, found our way out. We ran down the stairs and into the narrow street. We carried on running for another five minutes, looking behind us every so often to make sure we weren't being followed. Having not one dollar left for a taxi or bus (too late for the underground) we had a long trek back to Larry's flat. By the time we arrived and slumped into bed it was after five and getting light.

When we roused ourselves around noon the next day – a Sunday – we had regained our cockiness and discussed our "escape" in bragging terms. But that lighthearted view of our experience rapidly disappeared when I received a further shock. I found I had lost my bunch of keys. My flat key, locker key, school keys and my motorbike key – all of them on a single bunch. Without them I was paralysed, and what made the situation worse was that I had a pretty good idea where I had lost them.

The thought of finding the Golden Dragon was bad enough. But the thought of having to go back – assuming I had left my keys there and that they had found them and that they were willing to let me come and fetch them – was definitely disconcerting. I would probably be threatened with physical violence and forced to pay back the extortionate bill. I didn't look forward to renewing my acquaintance with the Golden Dragon management and staff.

Nevertheless, I had no choice but to try and regain my keys. The first step was to work out where the Golden Dragon was. We had been worse the wear for drink and it was the middle of the night. We had no idea where we had been in Mongkok. Being pragmatic I consulted the telephone yellow pages. Larry was derisory of this effort, reflecting that a sleazy back street night club was unlikely to be listed.

There were dozens of Golden Dragon establishments, this name being auspicious and lucky in Chinese. There were Golden Dragon restaurants; Golden Dragon stores; Golden Dragon buildings – and then, yes, three Golden Dragon night clubs.

Step two was to summon up enough rudimentary Cantonese to articulate a few key phrases such as: "Did you find any keys?" "Do you have any keys?" "Can I come and get them?" Both Larry and I had learned some primitive Cantonese, but we needed a half hour's practice with a dictionary.

From the first Golden Dragon nightclub, I elicited no answer. As it was early afternoon, this was probably not surprising. I tried the second. Someone answered. I tried my Cantonese sentence. They slammed the phone down. I rang again, with the same result. This all looked pretty hopeless, but ever the optimist, I tried the third.

A female voice answered in Cantonese. I ventured my question again in what I thought was a fairly good tonal rendition of "Did you find any keys?" in my best Cantonese.

"What you want?" replied the lady in English, clearly recognising me for what I was and not bothering to continue any further linguistic torture. As clearly as possible I explained my problem. To my great surprise and relief, she told me they had found a bunch of keys on the floor and that they were probably mine as she seemed very aware that a couple of strange young expats had been in the club the night before. She told me I could come round anytime and even told me the name of the road, so I could find it on a street map.

With trepidation I ventured up the stairs of the Golden Dragon an hour later. My fear was soothed slightly by the fact that Larry had agreed to pay half the bill if we really had to, though this would have been a real setback for both of us. It was equivalent to a week's salary for me.

Compared to the vision of oriental eroticism of the night before, enhanced by dim lights, red velvet furnishings, and smartly dressed, heavily made up young women, the Golden Dragon in broad daylight was neither golden nor exotic. I found myself in a shabby bar, with threadbare red furnishings and a sticky floor. There was a faint smell of urine, incense and beer.

Behind the bar a middle aged Chinese lady was busying herself drying glasses and cleaning up. She was wearing a large grubby white apron and rubber gloves. Now she may well have been a triad, or at least a triad mamma, but I didn't feel threatened. Seeing no-one else there, least of all a thug wielding a Chinese chopper, I guessed I was safe enough.

"Ah, you come back! Lost your keys! Very silly boy!" said the lady and I realised that it was the selfsame Mama San who had given us a hard time the night before. She chided me, rummaged around behind the bar, and gave me my keys. She even managed a smile. Nothing was said about the bill or the money.

"Come back next time! Don't drink too much!" she said as I departed. That I found extremely ironic. I had suspected a triad ambush and finished up being chided by a Cantonese auntie.

So the adventure came to an anti-climactic but healthy conclusion. We had been to the pinnacle of Hong Kong social life; we had plumbed the murky underworld, all in a single evening. We had overcome social embarrassment and cultural clumsiness, as well as a menacing threat. We emerged a little the wiser for the experience. Just a little.

Grand Ol' Team to Play For

They said – but I suspect it was largely apocryphal, or wishful thinking on the part of the colonial dinosaurs still around – that there used to be a sign at the entrance of the club which read "No dogs or women." The Hong Kong Football Club, when I joined it as an enthusiastic amateur in 1978, was still a male dominated, expatriate oriented institution, but it had moved a little with the times. Women were definitely allowed.

Being sports-driven, it lacked the sophistication or status (or wealth) of the Hong Kong Club or the Jockey Club, or even the Ladies Recreation Club, and it wasn't so ethnically integrated as any of those examples, which were essentially social clubs.

The HKFC, as it was known, was populated mainly by Brits, with the occasional American, Aussie, European or Hong Kong Chinese thrown in, and it had a very British culture. Football as the name suggests, was the predominant offer, but Rugby, Hockey, Lawn Balls, Squash and Tennis were also on the agenda. It was in some senses an heir to the dreadful arrogant colonial clubs of the old days, and exuded a typical kind of British grammar school, local town club team spirit and chumminess, but by the time I landed, it was at least down-to-earth, unpretentious, and had a democratic spirit which determined people's status on the basis of their sports ability more than their race, ideology or financial ranking.

Such clubs, whether sporting or social in nature, were still woven into the fabric of Hong Kong life, especially expat social life, but the old racial prejudices and barriers were being broken down by the 1980s. Some clubs, like the Craigengower Cricket Club, had been transformed. By the late seventies it was managed by a Chinese administration, which had understandably converted the cricket fields into tennis courts and lawn bowling greens, both games being popular with the Hong Kong Chinese.

The Kowloon Cricket Club, similarly, catered for a strong Indian and Pakistani community and their strong sports – cricket, hockey and squash – reflected that make-up.

As well as being a sports club, with excellent facilities, including a 12,000 seat football stadium when I joined, the HKFC was a community facility, with restaurants, bars and a swimming pool. It was, for me and most members, a cultural haven; a respite from the fascinating but exhausting hurly-burly of Hong Kong's manic business and social life; a chance to relax in an island of British norms, where language, convention and custom were automatic and didn't require consideration or cause embarrassment.

I joined the HKFC within a year of arriving in Hong Kong, with the dual motive of playing football competitively and making like-minded friends. Football had always played a part in my life, and I had been brought up in a football culture. My father had been a successful local amateur star and I always wondered why, as a small boy accompanying him through our town, strangers would come up and shake his hand. He cultivated my interest by showing me yellowing newspaper clippings of his glory days. Here he was, being carried shoulder high from the field by his team mates after scoring a hat-trick to defeat our local rivals, Bedford Town, in the FA cup. There he was again, featuring in a stilted team shot of the Hertfordshire County team.

Small wonder I inherited a love of the sport, and a degree of my father's talent. Through school and university the weekly ritual of training and playing was a part of life. As well as the physical thrill and catharsis of playing a demanding, competitive and energetic game, football provided me with psychological healing after a week's work. Here was a mindless pastime, purely bodily, which purged my mind of the petty anxieties of work and relationships. All I had to do was help my team get the ball in the net and defend ours. Life was uncomplicated for 90 minutes. In addition, I could call upon some primitive male urges to better my competitors. The liberal minded teacher turned into a fearless midfield tackler for whom no challenge was too hard. A good way to channel those primeval aggressive instincts.

As well as the athletic side, the social aspect of football was also reassuring. The vocabulary and conventions of the changing room and post-match pub or bar were standard and comforting. Your background didn't matter. Nor your intellect or qualifications. Nor your job. The criteria by which you became "one of the lads" were based more on your ability to control the ball, score goals, tackle bravely and contribute untiringly to the team effort.

Conversation was essentially based on teasing one another, enjoying the "crack" and analysing the game just played, however unskilful, with intense and detailed punditry. It was more complex than discussing the weather, and required knowledge of the right phrasing and syntax, but no-one need be excluded, however unintelligent. It was into this comforting and unchallenging social world I joined in 1978 when I signed up for the HKFC.

In the same way that Hong Kong opened up avenues of opportunity in my career and social life, that I would likely not have encountered had I stayed living in the UK, it also provided me with unexpected and thrilling football experiences.

Having played at a good university standard and a reasonable amateur level in the UK I had no preconceptions of the standard in Hong Kong. After a two year break from playing, largely because of knee injuries, I wasn't even sure whether I could play regularly. However, after a season in the 4th and 3rd teams, I regained my fitness and confidence and graduated to the first team squad. So began a four year affair at the top echelons of the territory's football community.

Hong Kong football was professional at the highest level, first division teams comprising salaried or part-time paid players, mostly local Chinese. However, an incongruous foreign element had been injected into this scene in the 1970s. Some of the wealthy Chinese owners of the top clubs decided to boost their prospects by importing young professionals – and they first came from Scotland. As a result a crop of young talents, who may or may not have made it with Glasgow Rangers or Celtic, found themselves playing for Rangers in Hong Kong.

At that time the top teams in Hong Kong could attract crowds of 30 or 40,000, and some of the young Scots became celebrities among the Cantonese fans and in the media. They earned more than they would have done in Glasgow, and they certainly achieved local stardom.

Among them was Derek Currie, whose flowing dark locks and beard earned him the nickname of "Jeso" or Jesus among the Chinese, who thrilled at his electric pace down the left wing. Then there was Walter Gerrard, a powerful stocky centre forward who bulldozed his way past intimidated Chinese defenders into local folklore as "Sui Ngau" or "Buffalo."

Professional football was widely popular in the 70s and 80s in Hong Kong and almost matched horse racing for its high profile. Teams making up the first division were a mixed bunch, however. Some were pet projects of Hong Kong Chinese taipans; others were sponsored by brands, such as the watchmakers Seiko or Bulova; some, like the Police or Urban Services, were institutional in origin. Political loyalties underpinned a few, while geographic location – Tsuen Wan for example – determined some. At that time twelve teams formed the first division and each year two were relegated to the mostly amateur second division.

Into this heady mix the HKFC pitched its first team of purely amateurs. Occasionally in the past it had succeeded in gaining promotion and climbing into the professional ranks. This inevitably resulted in demotion at the end of the first season as the amateurs failed to match the fitness and skill levels of the pros.

But playing at the top level also had well recognised political as well as sporting implications. Being an entirely expatriate and amateur team we were not welcome as far as the Hong Kong Football Association was concerned. Understandably, they wanted to promote and build a strong local, Chinese based, professional league to a high standard that would attract and inspire Cantonese fans.

When a team of part-time amateurs – teachers, bankers, policemen and quantity surveyors – could compete in the first division, it was little short of embarrassing, as it suggested the professional standard was not distinguishable from the recreational version.

Graduating to the first team in 1979 as I did was fortunate, because a combination of factors created a talented group that year. First, we had three players who were undoubtedly of professional standard – a goalkeeper, a goal scoring centre-forward and a fast winger. Two of them did get paid for their talents later on. Second, we had a set of hard-training, capable amateurs to support them, whose commitment to the game extended beyond the bar (but didn't exclude it). Third, we had an ambitious and effective coach, whose talent lay in building a close knit, mutually supportive squad, generating enthusiasm for professional level standards and understanding how to use the resources available on the football field to maximum effect.

In our first season together we won the second division, so gaining promotion, and the Junior Shield, the cup competition for amateurs. This was my introduction to competitive football Hong Kong style. It took some acclimatisation. The heat and humidity – usually over 90% – was a challenge in itself. Salt tablets were used to replace the body's natural supply, which was quickly sweated out.

Dry, flat and dusty, most pitches were rock hard and required a high level of ball control and technical skill which the local Chinese players usually possessed to a greater degree than us. Most Hong Kong boys had grown up learning their football on asphalt playgrounds, with hard plastic balls half the size of a regular football. Unsurprisingly, they acquired great nimbleness and a sure touch on the ball. In return, us expats had, in general, more height, weight and a physical style, which we unhesitatingly used in the struggle for victory.

This cultural clash on the field of play normally led to nothing more than hard fought and sporting battles, sprinkled with the standard oaths and complaints aimed at each other and the referee. Occasionally, however, the competitive spirit boiled over and taking on unfortunate racial dimensions, turned into ugly confrontations.

One particularly ill-tempered match on Happy Valley disintegrated into a keystone cops farce. We had been alerted that these opponents were a "triad team" – probably hearsay – and braced ourselves for the rough tackles that ensued. Matters were already heated when the wife of one of our players watching the game from the touchline, made an unfortunate intervention. As their winger galloped past her she stuck out a foot and tripped him. He leapt up infuriated and pushed her over onto her backside. Nearby expat spectators rushed to her defense. The other Chinese players and their backup team immediately launched into the melee. Punches were thrown. Within seconds an almighty martial arts battle, which could have graced any Bruce Lee film, was underway.

Discretion took precedence over valour and our coach had the sense to summon us all – players and supporters alike – into a headlong tactical retreat back to the Football Club, a few hundred yards away. And so we ran, pursued by a hostile crowd, to the safety of our expatriate laager.

Such incidents were rare, however, and most games were played with mutual respect and enjoyment of the game. For amateur players some moments were especially memorable for us. When we played in the Junior Shield final (amateur cup final) at the Hong Kong Stadium, and emerged victorious, we relished playing in front of 30,000 noisy fans. Admittedly, they had mainly turned up early to enjoy the game following ours – the Senior Shield – but this in no way diminished our moment of popular fame. Afterwards, as we made our way up the stands to join our friends as spectators, we glowed with pride as Chinese fans patted us on the back. "Ho ye!" they shouted, "Well done!"

However, our most memorable sporting moment came at the end of our first season playing with the professionals in the first division. Training at least three times a week we pushed our fitness levels up to a standard which enabled us to match our opponents on most occasions. We scraped together enough points to make the avoidance of relegation possible. This possibility seriously disturbed the local football establishment and there was intense speculation in the media about skulduggery, bribery and match-fixing going on to make sure we dropped back where we belonged.

In the end, and with an irony that couldn't have been arranged, it all came down to the last game of the season. To stay up, we had to win. For our opponents on that day, a draw would have been sufficient to maintain their professional status – and their jobs.

Some 5,000 fans showed up to the Hong Kong Stadium to witness the fate of the gweilo team. To quell rumours of referee intimidation, a new referee was appointed at the last moment. This didn't prevent us from being outplayed for most of the game – yet somehow our opposition just couldn't score. With only five minutes remaining a goalless draw, along with our relegation, seemed inevitable.

But then, a bizarre moment changed everything. A harmless long shot was comfortably caught by their goalkeeper. As he steadied himself, our burly centre forward gave him a gentle, but provocative shoulder charge. Instead of ignoring it the Chinese goalie turned and kneed him in the crotch. Our heroic forward collapsed in a heap and with admirable thespian skill rolled in agony. Our referee, no doubt eager to express his impartiality and judgement, immediately gave a penalty kick. We scored, survived a final frenetic five minutes, and thereby created HKFC history by avoiding immediate relegation.

Avoiding relegation may not seem admirable to many football followers, and certainly not to non-footballers. But within our microcosm of Hong Kong football, we were, for a while, able to bask in glory, and the team, in the annals of the Club, were awarded legendary status.

The next season we managed to gain only a handful of points and were relegated back to the second division.

Playing for the HKFC first team afforded many pleasurable moments. Such as when I scored the winning goal in a key match, which was reported in the Hong Kong papers the next day under the headline "Wingate Upsets the League". These clippings were of course sent airmail to my father, who was undoubtedly proud. I also sent him a couple of clippings from the Chinese language press, in which I was referred to as

"Wan Guy Duck", (Wingate being hard to transliterate). He may have found these puzzling.

Before I stepped down from the first team – the demands of career assuming greater priority in life – I also played against some former heroes. Aging British stars often came out to Hong Kong to earn a few extra pounds in the twilight of their careers, to play for a season or even make a few cameo performances. Thus I found myself marking Alan Ball in one game. One of the 1966 World Cup winning English team, Ball could no longer run much, but was so skilful I failed to tackle him once or prevent him passing the ball.

As age caught up with me too, it was time to turn to social soccer at the Club, which offered plenty of opportunity to those whose love of the game outlived their youthful ability to play it properly.

The Club was as important to me for its social life as for its sporting offer. As I never married until my late thirties, I used the Club as a second home while a bachelor. There was always to game to look forward to, with the inevitable gatherings and analyses afterwards. There were functions and squash matches and there was always the bar. On an empty weekend, when one's social diary was empty, and one's latest girlfriend had walked out, or been tactfully deserted, the HKFC bar offered that bland, warm, cheerful environment for group therapy between fellow bachelors.

We shared highly original thoughts about the latest games in British soccer; moving on after several bottles of San Miguel or possibly Tsingtao beer into our own theories of running the national team. After a couple more we may have ascended up to the intellectual heights of political discourse or indeed metaphysical philosophy, though we probably didn't call it that. A few more and the debate would crash back to earth with personal revelations of heartbreak or lust. Finally, as the night drew on, and intoxication drew its misty veil over us, we would head off down to Wanchai, where the bars where in full swing until the early hours.

However, the social highlights had to be the HKFC tours. Twenty or thirty hardy, dedicated footballers, most beyond their better years, would bedeck themselves in smart Club blazers, ties and grey slacks and set out to grace the soccer fields of Asia and beyond. A certain juvenile madness would overcome us on leaving Kai Tak airport, particularly the married players, at the thought of a few days unfettered male carousing, but I'm pleased to report the boisterousness and affected macho behaviour was usually confined to our own ranks and not inflicted in public on the gentler Asian cultures we visited.

In fact, the tours I joined, as well as providing very challenging soccer and partying, gave this newcomer to Asia some memorable insights into the countries we visited.

Singapore, steaming and sultry, introduced us to soccer played in 36 degrees centigrade on the historic Padang, where we suffered with heavy hangovers. But it also opened its arms to reveal the historic Raffles hotel, the food stalls and Bugis Street. Here the transsexuals paraded in their finery, until the street was shut down by the prudish government, then re-opened again because the tourists missed it. Who could ever forget the first taste of fish head curry, washed down with cold Tiger beer on Boat Quay, on a humid, oppressive Singapore night?

On to Bangkok, where we played at the famous Royal Bangkok Jockey Club, and were entertained by a grim looking Thai general. That is grim, until the meal was finished and he regaled us with crude jokes, despite the elegant Thai ladies present. He was most amused by one of our party's rendition of "Barnacle Bill the Sailor" which obviously had some resonance with Siamese culture. But then, he also loudly applauded another effort – Elvis Presley's "I Wanna be your

Teddy Bear." Naturally, we had to drop in at Patpong and Soi Cowboy, the city's famous red light areas, during our stay.

One year we set off for Japan and Korea. Tokyo didn't excite me. I found it to be a characterless modern city, but Yokohama was more interesting and we played some well-matched football there against hospitable teams. Our Japanese hosts enjoyed the beer drinking culture of the game as much as us.

Then to Korea, where we were treated as celebrities. It appeared that we were mistaken for the Hong Kong national team, whom we resembled only in so far as we were well dressed in team uniform. On arrival, we were driven to the British Embassy for a drinks reception and formally greeted by the British Ambassador and the President of the Korean Football Association.

We did nothing to disabuse our hosts of their misperception of us and as a result, found ourselves lining up against their top university side the following day, under the intimidating scrutiny of national TV cameras. Several thousand fans looked on as national anthems were played, banners and many bows exchanged and speeches of welcome delivered.

Not surprisingly, as rather jaded versions of the youthful athletes we had once been, the sight of our super-fit, rugged and skilful opponents filled us with apprehension. This was a game for damage limitation and ultimately we did well, keeping the score down to an almost respectable 4-0 defeat.

One of the highlights of the trip, in between the football and drinking, was a visit to the de-militarised zone between North and South Korea. The frost laden terrain, swept by an icy wind, was bleak, and the tension, as the soldiers of both sides viewed each other with edgy suspicion, was palpable. It was an unforgettable scene, monument to a bitter historical conflict that defied resolution.

This type of cultural insight was an attractive part of our HKFC tours, which gave me and others an introduction to countries we had never visited before. Hence a tour to Australia a couple of years later was appealing, involving a visit to Sydney. We had a chance to take a boat trip around the famous harbour, admire Bondi beach and the Opera House, as well as drive along the Gold Coast.

Our games in Sydney were eventful. We landed at eight in the morning, after a boozy night in Singapore and not much sleep. This didn't seem to matter, as our first match was scheduled for eight in the evening, which would have allowed us to catch up on our sleep at the hotel. Imagine our dismay on being met at the airport by our hosts, the Sydney Bronco's, whose professional under-18 team we were due to face, and being told that, owing to floodlight failure, the game had been re-timed for eleven o-clock that morning, just three hours later.

A dishevelled, bleary-eyed squad – average age around 35 – appeared at the ground on time to take on the Bronco's finest young bucks. Somehow, and partially due to unlimited substitutions, we held them to a 3-2 win, which we instantly heralded a moral victory.

Our second game was arranged against Sydney's Croatian club. On arrival, as we disembarked from the team bus, our hosts expressed disappointment that we were not Chinese, assuming we were Hong Kong's national team.

"Ah!" one of them exclaimed, "At least you've one Chinese!" pointing to one of our team. "Oh no!" we had to explain, "That's just Duggie. He's Scottish and just looks oriental after a particularly heavy night last night!"

The Croats beat us 4-0, but at least we gave some respectable resistance in their impressive stadium. Afterwards they spoiled us with a fine dinner and much hearty drinking. What impressed them most of all, however, much more than our football ability, was our club song.

Having given our traditional after match rendition of "It's a Grand Ol' Team to Play For, And it's a Grand Ol' Team to see", etc etc. They eagerly insisted on learning the words and I believe they reproduced their own version. Whether that was in English or Serbo-Croat, I will never know. This song was once played at matches of Scotland's famous Celtic team. It was adopted, in diverse forms, by other British clubs and found its way to Hong Kong.

I sang, or heard it, many times over the years I was an active member of the HKFC, sometimes after sporting triumphs, and sometimes after loss, when it helped deal with the disappointment. It was something peculiar to British sporting culture, and the HKFC reflected that culture,

But, being based in Hong Kong, the Club also mirrored the cosmopolitan nature of the place – its openness and sense of adventure. Like Hong Kong itself, membership of the Club rewarded me with comradeship, lifelong friendships, good health, travel and a sense of adventure and fun.

By the time I left Hong Kong, if there were any signs outside, they would have been celebrating the diversity and inclusiveness of the club's community.

Chickens' Feet and Scorpions

My earliest encounters with Chinese food were uninformed and uninspiring. In my home town in North Hertfordshire, the first exotic foreign restaurants to appear were Chinese, probably the most exciting culinary development after Wimpey bars had first offered a taste of America with hamburgers and coffee. Two opened quite quickly in the 1960s, serving an eclectic mixture of anglicized Chinese dishes, curry and fish and chips.

The down-to-earth townspeople weren't that impressed and I can remember my father, having been dragged along unwillingly to sample the fare, declaring judgementally that it was insubstantial and left him hungry. He preferred the steak and chips at Bernie's Inns when he wanted a good night out.

For us teenagers though, the Chinese restaurant served a particular purpose and provided a welcome alternative to the standard chip shop. Its specific social function was to provide nourishment and entertainment in the interval between the pubs closing at 10:30 pm and the last bus leaving an hour later for the village where we lived.

We would troop, rowdy and tipsy, into the Yellow River restaurant, having consumed six to eight pints of bitter in two hours hurried drinking, and order what we considered to be sophisticated Asian dishes. The standard orders revolved around fried rice, special noodles, chop suey, prawn curry, spring rolls, sesame toast and sweet and sour pork. These were either completely unauthentic (prawn curry and sesame toast?)

or made up for what was considered desirable for the barbaric British palate (chop suey and sweet and sour pork?). All were invariably sweet and liberally doused in monosodium glutamate. In retrospect I admire the stoic performance of the Chinese waiters, who would have to deal with their slovenly clients and such sophisticated requests as: "Gi'us a beef curry mate and a plate of prawn crackers".

There was also the takeaway version, when you ate your noodles or prawn curry out of a styro-foam container with a plastic fork while sitting on a bench at the bus stop. This was a relatively glamorous experience, because you didn't eat it out of a newspaper with your fingers, as with cod and chips. I was rather restricted in this style of late-night dining, because, being a school student still, I was the poorest of our small band of aspiring bon viveurs. With my barely survival level of pocket money, I could usually only afford the cheapest takeaway dish of all – plain fried noodle. It was just about edible with a liberal sprinkling of soy sauce, but no doubt blunted the development of the finer senses of taste, and marred my induction into one of the world's great cuisines.

There was another obstacle to being introduced to the almost unlimited delights of Chinese food – prejudice. My parents, along with many of their generation, regarded Chinese food, and indeed the Chinese race, with suspicion. Repeating what my sister and I regarded as falsehoods and racist calumny in the conservative media, they talked in horrified tones about dogs and other forbidden meats being found in Chinese restaurants. As progressive, enlightened neo-Marxist teenage intellectuals we strongly denied these claims as pure bourgeois scaremongering. Little did I know!

One of the first steps in learning to appreciate Chinese food on settling in Hong Kong was to discover the pleasures of dim sum. Literally meaning "little hearts", but more precisely "tasty morsels" dim sum comprises of a range of small dishes, traditionally eaten by the Chinese at "yum cha" – light meals for chilling out and gossiping at any time of day.

In Hong Kong restaurants dim sum is normally served from trolleys being wheeled around tables by elderly ladies. This lets the customer pick and choose and experiment from the variety of foods. At first this could be bewildering, as the dim sum ladies rarely spoke English, so, unless you had the benefit of Chinese friends or long term expat colleagues helping, you just tried your luck.

You could say that certain dim sum were more accessible for expats and more obviously edible. For example, perennial expat favourites are "ha gau", "siu mai" and "char siu bao". Ha gau is a small crescent shaped dumpling, stuffed with prawn. It is incidentally, on account of its shape, also Cantonese slang for moustache. Siu mai is made of pork and char sui bao is a slightly larger pastry bun, flavoured with roast pork.

But if these were examples of "euro dim sum", there was another level for those with adventurous palates. Popular among the Cantonese were turnip cake, small pork spare ribs, cow's stomach, chickens' blood and chickens' feet. I always thought of the latter as a sort of rite of passage for those of us who considered ourselves as trans-cultural expats.

Eating chickens' feet symbolised two features of the Cantonese attitude to food – not wasting anything and enjoying meat on the bone. Apart from the psychological barrier expats experience about eating "fong zhao" or "phoenix claws" as they are called, the manner of eating means overcoming another cultural hurdle. Fong zhao are lifted to the mouth with chopsticks and bitten off into manageable mouthfuls. With skilful synchronised use of the tongue, lips and teeth, the delicious meat is teased off the small bones. Once these are sucked bare, the remains are then delicately deposited on the table – or simply spat out more normally. This is quite acceptable, and, in fact a degree of debris on the table is quite rightly regarded as positive evidence of a convivial meal.

A Chinese colleague of mine once related a chickens' feet tale. As a student studying in Birmingham, in the UK, he sorely missed his Cantonese food, and decided to find and prepare some real chickens' feet. He took the train to London, located a market where chickens' feet could be bought and returned in triumph.

Back in his student house, which he shared with three English girls, who were all away that weekend, he happily cooked his fong zhao in the frying pan. The results, he recounted, were tasty, but rather odd, for the feet were extra-large and the oil turned them black in stir frying. He ate three and put two in the communal fridge. This was unfortunate, for he forget to tell anyone. Late that night, he was woken from his sleep by a blood curdling scream. One of his female housemates had innocently opened the fridge only to be confronted by what she assumed were the dismembered and decaying hands of a murder victim.

I also enjoyed the mini spare ribs, or "pai gwat", which required similar dexterity in the mouth to enjoy properly, as well as lack of inhibition in dealing with the small bones. Very early on I also discovered my perennially favourite Chinese dim sum desserts – egg tart and mango pudding. Neither of them are traditionally Chinese but that didn't matter. Egg tart or "daan tart" in Cantonese, are individual egg custard tarts and mango pudding is a mango custard, usually served with tinned condensed milk. Definitely something to do with British culinary influence and one of the rare instances worth recording.

An early and pleasurable experience was to immerse oneself in the ambience of real neighbourhood Chinese restaurants. How far removed were they from the draughty, soulless, drab versions I had patronised in North Hertfordshire.

A genuine Hong Kong restaurant is full of colour, life and noise – too much noise sometimes!

For the Hong Kong Chinese, the restaurant is the preferred venue for business and family socialising. This is partly because Hong Kong homes are commonly small flats, and partly because they are private sanctum of the family. Only close relatives and intimate friends might be invited round.

Vast though many are, Hong Kong restaurants always seemed to be packed out and frequently you just waited patiently for a table, standing immediately behind the people most likely to be settling up soonest. This wasn't regarded as rude but common sense.

Tables accommodating ten or even twelve people were normal and this meant entire families, spanning three or four generations, or whole groups of friends, would gather to share the dishes and conversation. Compared to the stuffiness of traditional British upmarket restaurants, how refreshing it was to experience this mixture, where aged grandparents sat with their offspring, down to the newborn, who would be perched on high stools, or, more usually, crawling around under the table.

Imagine a vast hall, full of the hubbub of these tables. Add to it the clatter and clicking of crockery and chopsticks, the barking of the senior waiters directing operations, the crying of small children, the laughter of gangs of teenagers and you get something of the exuberant commotion of these places.

Staff were in a constant state of motion and always appeared to be unsmiling and bad-tempered. They would throw down the crockery and cutlery with a great show of exaggerated speed and impatience, and snatch away your dishes and rice bowls unfinished if you neglected them for a moment. Though this seemed rude at first you came to realise that this was just local style. To show you face and politeness as a customer, waiters didn't deign to interfere in any way with your socialising, and the quicker they got in with the job, with the minimum of intrusion, the better. Of course, when expats bothered to learn some Cantonese, it would prove an ice-breaker with even the most surly waiter.

I wonder to this day how these restaurants work so efficiently. The menus were limitless, while the numbers of diners could run into the many hundreds at any one time. Yet in Hong Kong you would be inclined to grumble if the dishes took longer than ten minutes to arrive. I have peeped into the kitchen of this type of restaurant and witnessed an amazing scene of organised chaos, heat, noise and activity, mirroring the action the other side of the swing doors.

In this good-natured but apparently anarchic environment, the new expat soon learned a few basic rules of survival. The first was to handle chopsticks with confidence and dexterity. Not just to pick up the obvious, like chunks of chicken, but to pincer slippery wedges of mushroom or grip slimy slivers of sea food. Otherwise, you would simply miss out. As a Chinese girlfriend explained early in this dining adventure, there were only two types of people at a Chinese meal – the quick and the hungry.

The second lesson was not to eat too quickly, for the range of dishes would roughly equal the number of you, ten or so, around the table. By digging in to the early dishes too greedily, you would simply lose out when the later delights turned up. Another rule – Chinese dishes come at once or as soon as they are ready, with the rice and noodles arriving last! The ballast of the meal comes at the end.

What a joy to eat so communally! You all share the food and dip into whatever dishes you like. If you are polite of course, you will make sure your neighbour, friend, or colleague next to you is served first, by offering them a morsel. How dull it soon seemed to eat just two or three dishes, on your own, in the formal European style, without trying anyone else's? What's more the traditional round table format means you enjoy the general conversation of the whole group, rather than possibly being limited to the bore on either side or opposite you when seated at a rectangular table.

Chinese eating is simply more fun. Rather than worrying about ridiculous petty points of etiquette, like eating your peas on the back of your fork, or using the right cutlery, the Chinese approach is to serve your friends or guests first, but, otherwise, there's little fuss. A successful Chinese meal might leave the table littered with prawns shells, chicken bones and other detritus, but this is seen as the sign of satisfaction. Anyway the waiters simply fold it all up in the paper table cloth and whip it away, then lay another for the next shift.

Most expats managed all this with no problem, but I would chuckle to see the prim and proper trying to pick up their rice from their bowl with chopsticks. Most of it would end up on the table or in their laps. Much better to use the Chinese method of lifting the bowl to mouth and elegantly brushing the rice in with the chopsticks. Not for nothing are chopsticks called "fai jee" in Cantonese – or "fast eat".

I always fancied myself as a broadminded, non-squeamish, man-of-the-world eater, and happily experimented with the exotic and outlandish. But with Chinese food there were limits. For example, I couldn't get on with dog. It was illegal in Hong Kong, though I understand it could be acquired. Sorry, Dad, you were right. I tried it in Mainland China, but found it too gamey. There was also a degree of Westerner's guilt involved.

Jellyfish and sea cucumbers also failed to titillate my palate. Jellyfish was frequently served in long strips as the decorative embellishment of the dish. Affectionately nicknamed "rubber bands" they were tasteless and very chewy. I also struggled with sea cucumbers and sea slugs. It wasn't so much the psychological barrier and the look of the food as the texture and taste.

On the other hand I enjoyed snake, which is like a strong-tasting chicken, and eel, with its greasy flesh. I also had no problem with fish being served whole, though the vacant eyes staring up from the plate could be disconcerting on occasions.

One traditional test of expat culinary acclimatisation in Hong Kong was a visit to the famous pigeon restaurant on Lamma Island. Here you were served a big dish of whole cooked pigeons, head and all, which you were invited to rip up and devour by hand. Bones were sucked clean and dumped on the table. Quite fiddly but very tasty, and washed down with cold Tsing Tao beer.

I was lucky enough to share a particular, expensive delicacy, eaten to a specific ritual with a Chinese family. This was the Shanghai hairy crab or mitten crab. These small fresh water crabs, the size a big hand, with their distinctive hairy claws, are sought after for their flesh and especially for the female roe. Coming to maturity in late summer, they are very expensive and much desired in Hong Kong. According to the ritual, you eat the male first and then systematically, the female, culminating in the roe itself. Each stage is accompanied with a different rice wine. Not being a crustacean devotee, I found the taste agreeable but not outstanding. The experience with my generous hosts was unforgettable though.

It struck me very early on in my Hong Kong life that our Western squeamishness at certain Chinese foods can't be moralistic. The Cantonese are well known within China for "eating everything with four legs except the table", but it's hardly strange that a culture which periodically endured deadly famine and overpopulation, right up to and including the Maoist era, would not waste any food whatsoever. Isn't there an environmental lesson here also?

Hong Kong offered some of the finest Chinese cuisine in the world. One could dine at exclusive restaurants and sit through 12-course "Imperial Banquets" at work functions or Chinese friends' weddings.

But I found the street-side and neighbourhood fare equally appealing. In the 1980s food stalls, both licensed and illegal, were still common. My favourites were in Wanchai, the red light and bar area, main night time haunt for the young, and not-so-young, drinkers and revellers.

Using the fierce heat generated from dangerous looking gas canisters, which produced a roaring flame like a furnace, the stall holders could knock up in an instant tasty noodle and rice combinations with their huge woks and choppers the only visible implements. Customers would perch precariously on wobbly plastic stools and eat from plastic bowls just yards away from the busy passing traffic.

My favourite time to eat at these places was late at night. Invariably, in my bachelor days, after an evening's drinking and socialising at one or several of the clubs in the area, we would find our way to the stalls after midnight. The strong smells of rapid, high heat cooking; noise and chatter of the late night crowd, gossiping, flirting, mixed with traffic sounds; all merging in the hot, humid Hong Kong air, created a seductive atmosphere. It was so exotically Hong Kong and Asia.

As an antidote to the evening's alcohol intake the food was perfect. I usually chose one of the noodle soups. A bowlful of thin, al dente egg or rice noodles in a strong soup base, topped with won ton dumplings and liberally laced with chilli oil. This was often accompanied by a dish of fresh, green choi sum or gai lan, Chinese cousins of spinach, flavoured with oyster sauce. Cost in those days? Five Hong Kong dollars – about 50 pence.

Alternatively, you could opt for beef balls or fish balls, being mashed meat or fish flesh rolled up into a ball the size of a conker. Most fish balls were, so the saying went, made in the notorious Walled City in Kowloon, the jerry built monstrosity of an illegal structure where through some quirk of history the British Government's writ did not run, and where criminals operated unmolested! Cantonese slang for a type of prostitute was also a "fish ball girl", because their skills at stimulating their customers resembled those of a worker hand manufacturing the tasty morsel!

If the Wanchai stalls, sadly now swept away in the historical tide of Health and Safety, were a main attraction at night, many small noodle shops provided an early morning equivalent. For a refreshing start to the morning, before heading to the office, you could do no better than enjoy a bowl of "chan daan mien." This simple dish consisted of instant noodles in a soup, on which was a slice of luncheon meat, a fried egg and a stick of choi sum. It was a sort of East-West fusion, which was nutritionally of dubious quality but packed with the necessary calories to fuel the body at the start of the day.

Other basics included the seafood offerings of the Lamma island quayside restaurants – a favourite destination for expat boat trips – where you chose your meal as it swam or crawled around large aquariums. Even fried rice, prepared at the most modest village family food stalls in the New Territories, washed down by more ice cold Tsing Tao beer, was delicious. Flavoured with garlic, spring onion, ham and prawns, it was a welcome finale to a day's hiking in the over 30 degrees, high humidity Hong Kong climate.

A large part of the secret of the flavouring for all this down-to-earth Cantonese food is the simplicity of its cooking. As a self-respecting cultural voyeur I obviously had to try and learn some of its essentials.

My chance to acquire some knowledge of Cantonese cooking – and I was starting at rock bottom, because the only Chinese food I had ever prepared came from boil-in-the-bag – presented itself when I met the delightful Bonny Cheung.

With her slender figure, long eyelashes, luxuriant hair and bewitching smile, Bonny captured my heart. I dated this ex-Cathay Pacific air hostess for about a year, before she had the sense to return to her more mature, reliable and wealthier boyfriend. In the meantime, however, Bonny taught me some basics of cooking with the chopper and the wok. I emerged from the relationship broken-hearted but with improved culinary skills.

My alluring tutor cooked with me, showing me several dishes, but it was the overall principles that were important. She demonstrated how all the ingredients needed preparation before even lighting the stove. Everything must be washed thoroughly and chopped up into at least bite size pieces.

The rice has to be sluiced three of four times to rid it of the dust and powder that will make it too sticky. Water, the level of which is to be one finger knuckle over the top of the rice, is salted and boiled. Once boiling the heat is turned down to a minimum, so the rice absorbs all the water through gentle simmering until it is dry. You can of course cheat and use an electric rice cooker these days.

For the main cooking all you need is a wok. In this you can stir fry, simmer, boil, steam and casserole. Modern woks might be Teflon coated, but traditionalists will swear by an iron one, burnt black with oil seared in over the years.

For stir frying, as Bonny taught me, the key thing is to get the oil really hot first, before throwing in the herbs and spices to "flavour the oil". These are many, but the "Four Kings" of Chinese cooking are chilli, ginger, garlic and spring onion. Once your oil is spitting and spiced you toss in your main meat or fish ingredients with supporting cast, stir vigorously so it doesn't burn, and the dish is cooked in the hot oil in moments. Result? Freshly cooked food with all natural flavours and nutrition sealed in. No extra animal fats (the preferred oil is vegetable extract) and no need for too much salt or sugar.

Of course, I simplify, and there's a huge range of other sauces and spices, such as the ubiquitous soy sauce, and oyster sauce and fish paste. The latter would – in its making – assault the nostrils with its pungency, as the shrimps and small fish dried in the hot sun out in the open at the old Star Ferry pier.

One Bonny lesson revolved around vegetables. Having grown up with the idea that cabbage, broccoli and other greens had to be boiled to near disintegration in salted water, it was revelation that vegetables could be cooked in a variety of tasty ways, without losing their freshness or crispness. Chinese spinach cousins such as choi sum and gai lan, just need a splash of soy, a pinch of shrimp paste and garlic or oyster sauce, while being turned in hot oil for a couple of minutes, to produce a delicious dish in their own right.

In tune with my failed attempt to retain the affections of the lovely Miss Cheung, the romantic culinary relationship also came to an abrupt halt. However, Bonny left me a legacy of the stomach, if not the heart.

My greatest test of Chinese macho eating came in Beijing in 1999, the year before I left Hong Kong to return to live in London. Chinese colleagues there were amused by the relish with which I tackled chickens' feet and other offal dishes. A challenge was in the air. Would I eat any Chinese delicacy? Naturally!

As a result scorpions were ordered and served. Now the recognisable shape of these nasty little creatures did turn my stomach momentarily, but this was no time to be fainthearted. Picking them up carefully one by one in my chopsticks, I closed my eyes before putting them in my mouth and chewing. An anti-climax really – they were anyway quite small and deep fried. They tasted rather like bacon flavoured crisps. I definitely prefer chickens' feet.

A return home to the UK meant no loss of interest in Chinese food for me and my family. I even went back to the

Yellow River in Hitchin, Herts, which had changed its name to The Beijing Palace. Intending to order some takeaway dishes, and showing off, I proudly ordered chickens' feet in Cantonese.

"Oh, sorry mate," said the young Chinese waiter, "I don't speak any Chinese. I was born 'ere, but you can chat to me Grandma if you like. She's out the back."

Naturally, they didn't serve chickens' feet either, but I did order some plain fried noodles, just for the hell of it. They hadn't improved much. Fortunately, there's always Chinatown in London, with authentic Hong Kong people cooking and serving real Chinese food. If they were just a little more impatient it would be even more authentic.

Sex in the City

In crude parlance they called it "yellow fever". It wasn't meant to be derogatory – but referred to the attraction Chinese women had for European men arriving in the Far East for the first time. Was it true? What did it mean? As a phrase it certainly wouldn't pass the test of political correctness, suggesting with outdated racial inaccuracy that Chinese are yellow, and also implying that being attracted by a Chinese woman was a kind of illness, you might recover from.

It stemmed from a colonial attitude, that lingered on, though starting to fade, into the years when I first arrived in Hong Kong in the late 1970s. I also suspect it was endorsed and promulgated by some European wives and girlfriends, who were concerned their partners heads might be turned by their Asian competitors.

It must be remembered that in 1978, the year I first stepped out of a plane at Kai Tak Airport, Hong Kong was still very much a colony, steeped in colonial prejudices. Mao had only just died. China was still a closed shop. And it would be some years before discussions about Hong Kong's future would begin.

These were the years when the dominant powers in Hong Kong were the great trading houses of Jardines and Swires, which, along with the Hong Kong Shanghai Bank, towered over the political and business landscape. As far as relations between the sexes are concerned, it's instructive to note that not many years earlier, those great companies frowned upon their young European bachelors marrying a Chinese woman. Having an affair, as long as it was discreet, was tolerated, of course. A mixed marriage, however, could lead to dismissal.

By the time I turned up, this no longer applied, but prejudices and misconceptions remained. It was, for example, perfectly acceptable to have a Chinese girlfriend and to marry her. There were many examples of successful unions. However, it was still unusual and awkward to see a Chinese man with a European woman.

Coming from the liberated "swinging sixties" in England, and not long emerging from my student days, I found Hong Kong's sexual mores old fashioned and took a while to understand them. At first, this was constrained by the fact I went to Hong Kong with an English girlfriend. However, we split up after nine months, largely owing to my enjoyment and exploration of the place, while she missed home. So began my bachelorhood in Hong Kong.

I did find Chinese women exotic and attractive, but I don't think I had any particular preference for Asian women over European women. It was generally the case that Cantonese women in Hong Kong were slim, petite and smooth skinned compared to Europeans, but it was probably the very difference of being foreign that excited curiosity.

The problem was that in Hong Kong most European women were married, while the singles were few in number. Many more young British males were out in Hong Kong working, than females. There was also a prejudice that British women out there were on the hunt for a wealthy British husband, for many young Brits working in finance, the trading giants, or even Government, were very well paid. These women were unkindly considered to be on a "fishing trip" in Hong Kong. At the same time their targeted prey were also slandered as "Filth" – a delightful acronym standing for "Failed In London Try Hong Kong".

The challenge for a red-blooded young male was how to find that elusive partner for life, or indeed, a companion for sex and socialising in this society. There were opportunities to meet European and Chinese girls through the usual social channels – i.e. clubs, parties, bars, boat trips. But it was certainly harder to meet Chinese women.

Chinese society itself in Hong Kong was also quite conservative in matters of sex. It was not necessarily accepted by many Chinese families that their daughter should marry or consort with a non-Chinese. And there was, at that time, still a language issue. Many young Chinese women spoke English, but not to a comfortable conversational level, while most of us expats were entirely useless at learning Cantonese. So it was not always easy to meet a Chinese girlfriend who would be comfortable in an expat social setting. Add to this a rather Victorian primness about sex was prevalent – a coy and puritan approach in public – along with a hypocritical toleration of libertarian sex, as long as it remained unspoken about and was carried on in the dark!

For young expats like myself there was plenty of opportunity to indulge in the sleazier side of sex. The bars of Wanchai were full and fun. They weren't anything like the world of Suzy Wong, as depicted in the famous novel, but they were quite relaxed and easy going. However, what most of us singles wanted was to meet a "good Chinese girl". Apart from work, it was quite difficult, because "good Chinese girls" didn't usually drink alcohol, so didn't go to bars or consort with foreigners.

I didn't regard myself as a victim of "yellow fever", but, being on my own, I did have a need for a steady girlfriend, at the very least, and I did find Chinese women alluring. I'm sure I shared the prejudices of many young expat males in this respect.

Bonny Cheung was a former airhostess. Modern, well-travelled, sophisticated and fluent in English, she was not a typical Hong Kong woman of her age. But she was my first steady Chinese girlfriend and through her I experienced the complications of cross-cultural love affairs. Most of the hangups were, of course, mine. As much as I adored her, I was always conscious that I was the foreigner in Hong Kong on "borrowed time."

I wasn't even sure how long I would stay – my teaching job didn't seem to have a future – and I had always planned my Hong Kong adventure to last two years. Little did I know at that stage that Hong Kong would hold me for another 21 years! The net effect was to give Bonny the impression that this relationship was temporary and that I was shy of committing to anything long-lasting.

However, the year I spent with her was full of fun and happy times. Meeting Bonny in the first place hadn't been easy. In fact it was a blind date, set up by a friend of mine who was courting her airhostess friend. It was quite awkward and stilted at the beginning, though I immediately found her very attractive.

Another ridiculous prejudice I had was to be worried at the time that she would fit in with my expat circle of friends, although some of them had Chinese or Philippina girlfriends. This proved completely unfounded, but a longer-term doubt which did linger as our relationship progressed was the question of taking Bonny back to the UK if we were to stay together. This seems equally nonsensical in retrospect but it troubled me at the time.

Bonny had none of these concerns, but sensed my unease and resented my doubts. She moved comfortably in all social circles and I was very proud of her. She was charming and caring and my inhibitions irritated her.

We became lovers quite quickly, which surprised me, because I was assured Chinese girls were very conservative in these matters. Bonny was entirely uninhibited about sex, and love-making with her was affectionate, natural and relaxed. Now this could hardly be a generalisation about Hong Kong Chinese women, but I did gain the understanding that they were not necessarily quick to consent to sex, but once they did, they lacked any shyness or reservation about the act or about their bodies. Perhaps it was the absence of guilt which Christianity had associated with sex.

There was an eminently practical aspect to the relationship. Bonny, like other Chinese women I knew, was tender but not romantic. The Cantonese language doesn't contain any endearments and marriage was traditionally viewed as an arrangement ensuring companionship and family continuity. Not to get married, for a woman anyway, was the exception. Only "black and white amahs", who dedicated themselves to domestic service, and unfortunate spinsters, remained unmarried. Getting married and having children was the norm.

There was little recognition of the Hollywood western concept of "falling in love" or "love at first sight". Love and respect needed to be earned through showing fidelity, support, financial commitment and the acts of partnership were more important than the words. Partners needed to be "suitable."

My relationship with Bonny never reached the stage where we seriously discussed marriage or even permanence, but there was always a time element attached. Quite early on I was made aware that she wanted commitment in this relationship. She was 24 years old. I was 28. I remember her saying: "It's alright for you men. You are still sexually attractive until you are 48. But us women, we are on the shelf at 28!" I was struck – not only by the sentiment differentiating the comparative prospects of the genders – but by the precision of the judgement on age limits!

I was serious about Bonny and anticipated, at the very least, a long-lasting relationship. I assumed I was a reasonable catch for her – a teacher, single, healthy, and being European was itself an attraction. Being invited to meet her family was a clear, and unusual, sign of this seriousness. They were welcoming and I was obviously accepted as a decent partner for their daughter. I couldn't really converse with her mother and father, as they didn't speak English, and my Cantonese was primitive, to say the least.

However, my own hang-ups eventually spoilt this budding affair. First, I decided to attend the annual ball held by the international school where I worked, on my own. This was because I gauged it would be very stuffy and formal and I didn't want my colleagues to know too much about my private life. However, this was a major miscalculation, because Bonny assumed it was because I didn't think she could handle a formal European event. She thought I was embarrassed about her and lost face. She didn't talk to me for a few days and our relationship was damaged.

Then, after about a year together, I made another mistake. I planned to take a break during my schoolteacher's summer holiday. As my sister lived in Malaysia, I aimed to visit her and take a backpacker's tour through Thailand, Malaysia and Singapore. This would take a month and it seemed sensible to me to go on my own. Bonny was offended I was not going with her. I didn't realise just how much she was hurt until I returned a month later.

When I got back she told me it was all over. She was returning to her former boyfriend, about whom I knew very little. He was British – a successful, forty-year-old businessman. Bonny informed me he wanted to marry her and she wanted to have a baby. I was too indecisive, I was told. I couldn't offer the financial stability he could. This was devastating for me as it all seemed so calculating. But I loved her! Too bad, I hadn't shown her enough respect and I wasn't ready. However, the last time we were together, she "let me" make love to her as she wanted to leave me with something to remember.

I was heartbroken. I rationalised this as a result of my inability to understand the Chinese female psyche. There was an element of truth in that. Now I was a bachelor again. Of all the places to be single, at least Hong Kong was one of the most agreeable.

There were, in the early 1980s, some 120,000 Philippinas in Hong Kong. Working mainly, though not exclusively, as live-in domestic maids under rigorous contractual conditions, they made up the largest non-Chinese foreign contingent in the territory.

They were, simply, heroines; part of that Philippine diaspora that shames the feudal elite of that resource-rich country. As live-in maids in Hong Kong, they were contractually tied to their employer – good or bad though they may have been. They were bonded labour. If they broke their contract, or offended their employer, or simply fell foul of the boss, they could be sent home. Most earned around $HK3000 a month, plus food and lodging. Compare this with the average salary of a bank clerk in Manila – $HK700 – and you can understand the motivation to subject themselves to those conditions.

As the usual terms of employment meant these women had only Saturday night and all day Sunday free, it was no wonder the more free-spirited among them partied energetically. For us European bachelors they provided a welcome source of female companionship and fun.

Despite the gloomy shadow of Catholicism which hung over their country, providing another impediment to its progress, the Philippinas we would meet in the bars and discos of Hong Kong were in general optimistic and positive people, who rarely seemed to grumble about their situation. Many had a lot to complain about. Most seemed to have married young, fifteen or sixteen, borne children early and endured poverty. They sought an escape by finding work in Hong Kong, usually through exploitative agencies. If they succeeded their earnings were often remitted home to sustain their children and their extended families.

Another advantage for us British males was that Philippinas spoke English, and because of the US influence in their country, were familiar with popular English language culture. We met them on Saturday nights, when they enjoyed a respite from work, usually danced all evening, and were happy to have male company.

Some of my friends met and married Philippinas and their marriages have lasted well, with the family often staying in Hong Kong. But longer-term relationships faced many obstacles. Whilst they could be quite sexually liberated, and one-night stands were possible, it was difficult to sustain a regular partnership, given their working conditions. It meant the man had to make a full and complete commitment and undertake contractual responsibility for the woman. In short that meant getting married!

Otherwise, liaisons were limited to weekends. I had one Philippina girlfriend and lover I was very fond of. Joanie was a domestic helper – petite, vivacious and confident. But I could only meet her on Sunday evenings, and even then she would always have to leave by 11:00pm, in order to return to her employers, get enough sleep and start work at 7:00am in the morning. Selfishly, I would plead with her to stay overnight, but to no avail.

After some six months of this frustrating relationship, during which she was never in the least demanding of me, she gaily announced one Sunday evening, on departing, that she was getting married. She had met a "very nice" young Swedish man, who had proposed. I never saw her again. I bet the marriage worked.

My sometimes heavy drinking Football Club coterie of bachelors had a favourite disco bar popular with Philippina women – the Makati Inn. Named after a district of Manila, this bar was dark, humid, crowded and bedecked in the non-dancing area with a carpet that stuck to the soles of your feet.

It was always packed and heavy with cigarette smoke and the smell of stale beer. In this romantic atmosphere, us beaus would stand at the perimeter of the dance floor eyeing up potential partners, earnestly sipping endless glasses of San Miguel beer. The girls would gyrate monotonously to the repetitive beats of the latest disco sounds, and we would occasionally venture into the fray, ask someone to dance and hope to gain their attention. Most of us were unaccomplished dancers and the medium was merely a route to asking them to sit down with us for a drink, where the real seduction process could begin.

It sounds awful, but it was convivial, relaxed and undemanding. Sometimes we got lucky and met a partner for the night. Occasionally, we met someone we dated. And some of my friends fell in love.

The Makati Inn also had its moments of dark excitement. This usually involved drunk British squaddies pestering the women, looking to pick a fight with "locals" like us, or just as often with their colleagues. Such fisticuffs, horribly inept because the combatants were too inebriated, were always brought to a rapid and brutal conclusion by the red-capped Military Police, who would appear suddenly, beat the young combatants mercilessly with truncheons and hurl them downstairs to the entrance. The lights would be dimmed again, the music resumed, the hips renewed their swaying and we continued our rituals.

Such nights were invariably long. Most places stayed open until 3:00am and many until 5:00am. Often we would break up the long drinking sessions by eating noodles and spicy food at the street-side stalls that proliferated in Wanchai. If you lasted until five and still hadn't met the love of your life, it was time to resort to the South China Hand. Styled like a typical English pub, it stayed open 24 hours and served a full English breakfast.

Wanchai district had several disco bars like the Makati Inn. You could meet Thai girls sometimes as well, though they tended not to be domestic servants. What they did we never really knew but many were illegal entrants to Hong Kong, overstaying on tourist visas. Some were amateur weekend hookers. I say amateur, because they were not hard-nosed but very sociable and traditionally asked only for "taxi money."

Authentic professional prostitution also thrived in Hong Kong in various forms. Typically Hong Kong, which practised prudish double standards, it was accepted as an integral part of life yet never formally recognised or much discussed.

Its most obvious manifestation was in the "girlie bars" of Wanchai, the historic red-light area made famous in the Suzy Wong novel. Suzy Wong was the good-hearted whore who fell in love with her sailor client. From experience, I can say the ladies working in these bars were more businesslike than romantic Suzy.

Like many other young men I was curious about these bars in my early years. With names like the Panda Bar, Goldstar, Neptune and San Francisco, they promised eroticism, oriental mystique and adventure. In reality, they were really quite bland and predictable. Bored, but attractive Chinese women, topless, would sit behind the bar, making formulaic conversation in the attempt to get you to buy them a drink. Beer was normal priced but "Hostess Drinks" were £20 a shot, even in those days.

"What's your name?" and "Where you from?" were the standard opening gambits. If you remained resistant to this repartee, they would move on to another client at the bar, with a weary "No money, no honey!" Overseeing these establishments were formidable older female managers – the Mama Sans – who quickly dealt with any hanky panky that was not leading to a transaction, but encouraged it when it had a profitable outlook. They quickly sorted out the drunks or the pests.

Apart from wasting your money on the appallingly high drinks prices, you could also request to escort one of the ladies from the bar. This, however, would set you back at least another £300 "bar fine" – a fee to compensate the bar for removing one of their staff – in addition to whatever you could negotiate with the object of your lust. This was simply a financial step too far for mere mortals like myself, who were not money-laden Hong Kong stockbrokers or currency dealers. Our fun consisted of trying to convince the professional "hostesses" to meet us after work. Needless to say this was a battle between optimism and realism.

Tourists were drawn to these bars and some were cruelly fleeced. Having been suckered into getting drunk, the victim would be persuaded to employ his credit card ordering rounds of champagne or other expensive delicacies. They would suffer massive bills of thousands of dollars, as well as a bad head. Even if they appealed to the police, or the media, they won little sympathy and rarely got their money or pride back.

Some bars were internationally famous. In Kowloon, you could visit Bottoms Up, renowned for providing the backdrop for a fleeting scene in an early James Bond film. Then there was the Red Lips Bar, whose hostesses were never younger than fifty, yet quite prepared to offer sexual services and scrounge drinks. We frequented these places occasionally, for special events like stag nights, but they had a negative effect on my libido.

At the upmarket end were very expensive night clubs, like the Bboss in Tsimshatsui. I did experience it at a later, business phase of my career, as a guest of expense account-funded clients. The women in these clubs were beautiful, skilful courtesans, almost like geishas, and they were extremely expensive.

The girlie bars in Wanchai changed as the years passed. By the late eighties they were full of Philippina pole dancers, who transformed the bars from humourless last resorts into party bars, where we went just to drink beer and chat up the girls. As time wore on, however, and familiarity bred contempt, these girlie bars lost their allure and became rather sad and drab.

Some years later, whenever I walked with my wife and family to a restaurant down Lockhart Road in Wanchai, which was lined with these bars, I would just have to hope that I wasn't recognised and a shout of "Hello Prankie" would not upset my domestic calm.

In addition to the seedy side of life changing in the wake of social development, so too did the regular pub and bar scene, which was where us gallants attempted to meet "decent" young women. Whereas in the late seventies there were few regular pubs, such as the "Bull and Bear", serving mainly the finance boys and girls in Central District, by the late eighties a whole new swathe of trendy drinking and dancing places were emerging in the new nightlife area called Lan Kwai Fong in the Mid Levels district of Hong Kong island.

Here gathered the new international cosmopolitan elite of Hong Kong, the first generation of youngsters of the rapidly emerging Chinese middle class, with their overseas degrees and multi-lingual skills; the wealthy expat kids from the international schools; and the young, single expats working in finance and commerce. It was a heady sophisticated mix, fuelled by late nights, alcohol and no shortage of recreational drugs.

I found this scene hard work. Probably, in my mid thirties, I was simply outgrowing it all. Perhaps I wasn't sophisticated enough. I didn't find many of the ladies frequenting this type of bar particularly attractive. I couldn't bother to go through the rituals of flirting and conversation. People seemed unauthentic, posed, material and superficial. I think I preferred the raw down-to-earth seediness of the Makati Inn.

Then, in the early hours of one morning, during the Chinese New Year holiday in 1988, I walked into Hardy's bar, an incongruous addition to the Lan Kwai Fong hostelries, having an English folk bar theme. I was tired and a little drunk. On bumping into former teaching friends, however, I was introduced to a woman called Ursula. She was unusual, amusing, confident and talkative. We discussed teaching, Latin, languages and Hong Kong.

Two years later we married – and we still are. Sex in the City had finally led to Sex in the Home and a beautiful daughter resulted. Ursula is German. In the end, Yellow Fever was trumped by Teutonic Temptation.

Tiananmen Trauma

One of the most iconic photos taken in Hong Kong, which encapsulated that time of expatriate privilege and colonial indulgence, was taken by a photographer sitting astride the wall of the Hong Kong Football Club. It was during the emotional demonstrations after the Tiananmen Square massacre in 1989. Directed along the top of an eight feet high brick wall, it showed, on the one side, luxuriant and indifferent, bronzed expatriate ladies, lazing on sun-loungers by the poolside. On the other, in the street leading into Happy Valley, it pictured a vast sea of Hong Kong Chinese citizens marching in grim protest, their banners waving, against the government which would soon determine their fate. No other picture epitomised the impact of those June events so poignantly.

Of all places, Tiananmen Square – the square of the Gate of Heavenly Peace – was the scene of one of the most spectacular acts of government violence against its own people the world has ever seen. But when I had visited it some years before, as a wide-eyed expatriate living in Hong Kong, it had very much lived up to its name for spiritual serenity. It was vast, empty, windswept, awe-inspiring and resonant with history – full of the ghosts of China's epic and periodically tragic past.

I had flown to Beijing in 1981, having patiently waded through the bureaucratic quagmire restricting foreign visitors in those days. This involved interminable waits at the People's

Republic visa office in Hong Kong; then further weeks' delays waiting for the visa to be granted and then booking a flight. Finally I arrived alone, to stay at a local Chinese run hotel – there was little available for foreigners anyway. Having learnt some elementary Putonghua – the Mandarin of mainland China, as opposed to the Cantonese of Hong Kong – I aimed to test out my language skills and to see for myself the famous sights of the ancient capital.

I managed to make myself understood at the hotel and even to hire a bicycle. On this boneshaker I cycled all over Beijing, often with local children running behind me, shouting "waiguoren!" "waiguoren!" ("foreigner! foreigner!"). At that time visitors were rare, certainly those using a cycle rather than a black limousine with shaded windows. There were very few cars and everyone still wore the Mao style suits of plain blue or black. The city, devoid of neon, was unspoilt, but colourless, dusty and drab.

Tiananmen Square itself remained a highlight of the visit. How could a former history student not fill his imagination with the place where the emperors ruled from the Forbidden City with detached splendour; where western troops once marched in triumph to humiliate China after suppressing the Boxer rebellion; where Mao declared the People's Republic of China established in 1949, telling the Chinese people that they had now got up off their knees; and where the famous Great Hall of the People loomed imposingly?

When I visited, the Square was populated by a few scruffy Chinese soldiers and by litter, blown across the open spaces by a grit-laden cold wind. The whole place was grey, but grand and slightly menacing. Were those policemen really keeping an eye on me? At the same time there was the awkward, shy welcome of young people, not keen to be seen to be too friendly, but eager to practise their rudimentary English. Did I come from London? Did I support Liverpool or Arsenal?

Then, all those years later, when a warmer wind of change had swept over China, and when a deal had been struck between China and Britain over the future of Hong Kong, Tiananmen Square was once again to enter my consciousness and at the same time, shake the self-confidence of Hong Kong people to its core.

At first, in the optimistic early months of 1989, it seemed like a logical extension of Deng Xiao-ping's economic reforms. Following the death of Mao in 1976, the diminutive, wizened Deng, who chain-smoked Panda cigarettes, had emerged, been purged, then re-surfaced again to set China on the road to reform. The opening up of China, step by step, through the special economic zones, heralded a dramatic change of direction from the orthodox Maoism which had held China in its idiosyncratic thrall since 1949.

But the Communist Party still held an iron grip and the reforms were economic, not political. This had been clear from the sudden repression in 1980 of the "Democracy Wall" movement. Dissent, briefly blossoming like an echo of the Hundred Flowers episode of the 1950s, was crushed once more.

Then, in 1989, the students of China found their voices again. Protesting against the chronic injustices of official corruption and censorship, their opposition was boisterous and colourful, yet peaceful. Marches, demonstrations, speeches – China hadn't seen the like of it for many years. Rumours spread that some individuals at the highest levels of the opaque party hierarchy – like Zhao Ziyang – were supporting change. The government was tolerating debate. But was it listening?

In Hong Kong we watched in fascination and hope. Was China really on the brink of a democratic breakthrough of some kind? The students in Hong Kong, traditionally non-political, ambitious, materialistic, lent their support. A kind of euphoria crept through the media and through the people of

Hong Kong. It was grounded in the belief that perhaps, just perhaps, the China that was to inherit Hong Kong in 1997 may not be so bad after all. Perhaps the kind of rule of law and personal rights which had existed, albeit imperfectly, in the colonial enclave would be allowed to flourish. Perhaps change was coming and a future guaranteed.

In Hong Kong we watched on TV, entranced, night after night, as the story unfolded. More students encamped on Tiananmen Square. Soon it was a seething sea of protesters, with their tents and sleeping bags, banners and flags, posters and slogans – optimistic, cheerful and confident. This was a true mass movement and it seemed that the population of Beijing was supportive, creating that rare and revolutionary coalition of students and workers that has shaken establishments around the world. Meanwhile, the Party seemed paralysed and the army invisible.

The army, however, was gathering, being put into position around Beijing, and in the days of May it began to move. Optimism and carnival protest gave way to anxiety and fear as People's Army columns of tanks and troops began to advance cautiously along the straight boulevards leading through the suburbs direct to the Square. It was clear the patience of the party leaders was wearing thin.

But hope rose again, as a miracle happened. The people of Beijing, the workers, the office people, the drivers, teachers and all, swarmed from their homes in the side streets and hutong alleys in their hundreds of thousands to jam the streets and engulf the tanks and troops with the sheer weight of their numbers. In most places it was tense but amicable. But in others there was violence and some soldiers and civilians lost their lives.

The masses had risen up and created a standoff. This played out on Hong Kong TV, where we all, locals, expats and visitors, debated the outcome and weighed up the options.

What did this all mean for us? The possible outcomes had vastly different implications depending on your statehood and economic status.

On the evening of June 4, 1989 I was in a restless mood. My life was changing. I was waiting for the return to Hong Kong of my girlfriend, soon to be my wife. We had been apart for a year. My bachelorhood was coming to an end. I also owned a flat, which I had bought three years before. Buying property in Hong Kong in those years was quite a risk, with the colony's open border economy subject to massive upswings and slumps. Now the political tension added to this uncertainty.

In the early evening I had played squash at the Hong Kong Football Club, one of the traditional expat hangouts, my home from home, and took a meal with friends there. I wasn't paying any attention to the news. Later we headed, as often, down to Wanchai, the night-life and red light area of Hong Kong. The evening deteriorated into a long drinking session and the humid evening hours slipped by. One by one my drinking mates also parted, returning to wives or girlfriends or just a welcoming bed. At about four in the morning I found myself, wilting from alcohol and fatigue, slumped on a bar stool in a near empty club, incoherently trying to strike up a conversation with a disinterested and bored bar girl.

Just as I was summoning up the resolve to pull myself together and head for home, a friend of mine strode in. A journalist with the English language South China Morning Post, he had been on the graveyard shift, putting the last edition "to bed". Having completed his work he was looking for a recreational beer or two and by chance chose the bar where I sat.

I noticed immediately on greeting him, happy for some company, that he was not only sober but unnaturally serious.

"What's up?" I asked. "Something wrong at work?"

"You could say that," he replied in his lugubrious Burnley accent. "The bastards have sent the tanks in and they say that thousands are being killed!"

Knowing exactly what he was talking about and sobered by the seriousness of the moment, I jumped up and fell off the bar stool. After a last beer with my non-communicative friend I went home and immediately switched on the TV.

The scenes portrayed repeatedly in the early hours of that morning will always stay with me. Confusion, terror, violence. Tanks charging towards the Square. Weeping, hysterical interviewees. Mangled and bloodied bodies being carried in panic into hospitals. The detritus of the occupation in the Square. Torn, flattened tents and banners, litter and other rubbish. It was daylight before I slept and my sleep was fitful, the images of the massacre flashing through my mind like some video loop of a horror film.

In the cold light of the next day, the tragedy seemed worse. Miserable, tired and hungover my first thoughts were entirely personal and selfish. What did all this mean to me? As an expat I was lucky enough to have options. This wasn't my country or my problem. But I was affected. It was clear that if the political situation in China deteriorated into chaos, Hong Kong would suffer, particularly at this sensitive stage of discussions between Britain and China. My first thought was for my partner. She had been in Europe and was due to join me within weeks. We planned to get married. Should I tell her to postpone the trip? Perhaps there would be turmoil in Hong Kong and I would have to leave the place in a hurry.

I thought also of my flat. I had bought it two years before as part of a decision to commit to Hong Kong for some years more and it had been an expensive investment for me. Now it could prove a costly burden. Hong Kong property prices were volatile at the best of times. Now if it was worthless, I had lost all my savings and would have to start again. They were melancholy moments but I felt resigned rather than desperate.

Meanwhile, as I shrank into my own small world, the news storm surged on. For the international media this was a major moment in history – a potential turning point. How many had been killed? What had happened to the protestors? Did this presage revolution in China? Did it mean factional strife in the Chinese Communist Party? Would civil war follow? How would this affect the handover of Hong Kong?

There were strong rumours that the Peoples' Sixth Army – assembled from the distant provinces of China, loyal to the hardliners and brutal – had committed the atrocity. Meanwhile the local Beijing detachments, which had been held back by the surge of the masses in the streets, had been ordered to stand aside. If the army divided and infighting began, mayhem would follow.

For the people of Hong Kong this experience was traumatic and visceral. Their secure world of making money, getting educated and enjoying the legal protection of British sovereignty was being undermined and their hopes for the future rudely shattered. The Chinese government had viciously turned on their own students and workers, who were only peacefully demanding reform. Many Hong Kong residents were refugees or children of refugees from communism, and to them this was further proof of the evil of the system they had fled in the first place.

At first, there was an atmosphere of numbed shock in the streets and workplaces as everyone awaited developments with deep anxiety. This mood soon gave way to an overwhelming sense of grief, loss and fear, as if a beloved patriarch had been lost to a dependent family. The certainties of existence were dismantled at a stroke.

Everyday life continued with its demands and responsibilities, exerting a welcome discipline and structure.

For me, in my work at Hong Kong's trade promotion body, the June massacre had a direct impact. As international press manager I now faced a barrage of enquiries from the world's press. Instead of fielding questions about trade figures, or Hong Kong industries, or the latest Hong Kong blockbuster toy, I now had to explain what was happening in Hong Kong. Journalists wanted to know how cross-border trade was affected and how investment flows were reacting. They were keen to find out how businesses were reacting and how people felt.

From a professional point of view it was a real challenge. First, it was hard to read the situation. For the days immediately after the events, no news came out of China and speculation ran wild. Some Hong Kong business and community leaders made ill-considered apocalyptic statements about China being set back fifty years; about the economy collapsing; about civil wars and martial law; even about Hong Kong's borders collapsing before a new wave of refugees. None of this came about and within a few weeks those same spokesmen were red-faced and hastily retracting their statements.

Within this environment, speaking on behalf of Hong Kong, myself and colleagues with media roles had to stress that life was going on as normal; that trade continued; and that Hong Kong was not on the brink of collapse. We had to relay calm and confident messages, whatever we felt inwardly, and assume a balanced position for our media contacts. Within a few days we were referring to the Tiananmen "incident" or "events" rather than "massacre". I'm not sure how much we prevented sensational stories circulating but at least we could counter some of the more extreme headlines. It was nerve-wracking but exhilarating work. It felt like we were on the front line of international news reporting, with all the responsibilities towards Hong Kong's reputation that entailed.

After a week or so had passed, and it became clear that there would be no civil strife in China, and that the hardliners had re-established their authoritarian rule in the People's Republic, fear and shock gave way in Hong Kong to mourning and growing anger. The mourning was directed at the hundreds, or possibly more than a thousand, that had been killed in the operation to clear the Square. This feeling was to manifest itself in vast public wakes, involving hundreds of thousands of people, marching and protesting in the streets, like gigantic versions of Chinese funeral processions.

I was caught up in one of the largest demonstrations one weekend after the tragedy. On my way to Happy Valley, I realised the traffic had been brought to a standstill, so I got out of the taxi and walked. Soon I was enveloped in the huge crowds, who filled every road surrounding the famous race course area.

All walks of life and ages were represented in the masses. There was a sea of banners, mainly of white cloth, festooned in black or red Chinese characters condemning the Chinese government and its actions, demanding justice and democracy. Photos of the victims were carried high. Many marchers wore white sashes or hoods in the style of a Chinese funeral, white, as opposed to black, being the colour of death and mourning. Young men wore white cloth or red bandanas, tied around their foreheads, with characters scrawled across the front. But the mood was sombre rather than confrontational at this stage. There was some shouting of slogans, but generally an air of sadness, with more tears shed than fists raised. This made the experience all the more moving, because these people were mourning the loss of hope, extinguished by their future government's callousness.

Carried along in the crowd, I was not noticed. No-one cared that I was not Chinese. I realised that all attention was fixed on the focus of this particular meeting – a series of six large photos of some of more prominent dissidents, who had been killed, set against funereal wreaths and propped up against the wall of a building. Incense sticks were burning around and piles of flowers and more wreaths were being left as marks of respect.

As the huge crowd swirled around this area, individuals were approaching in groups of four or five, to stand respectfully before the makeshift altar and bow from the waist three times in traditional fashion.

As I got closer, out of curiosity, I wondered if I should follow suit. After all, I wasn't Chinese. This wasn't my struggle and as an expat my presence might be resented. Weren't the expats handing the Hong Kong people over to this murderous government, abandoning them to their fate, having profited nicely from decades of lucrative ownership?

But I wanted to join in and to make at least a token gesture of support, so I stepped forward with others and expressed my respect for the victims. No-one around commented and I don't think anyone even recognised my presence.

A few days later the incongruity of being an expat in this charged atmosphere became even more intense. I was having a few relaxing drinks at the Hong Kong Football Club on a Saturday afternoon, along with other expat friends. The Club itself, though friendly and liberal enough, had traditionally been an expat social enclave, and, while changing and welcoming many Chinese members, still typified the cultural separation that still existed.

As we drank and gossiped, another huge demonstration was gathering in the centre field of Happy Valley immediately next door. People were streaming in from all adjoining roads to gather round a stage erected in the middle of the grassy centre. Amplified messages and slogans were booming out from loudspeakers and echoing around the steep Happy Valley slopes with their stacks of high rise buildings. The question soon arose in our small gathering – "Should we go over and join?"

"What for?" said the cynics. "It's not our battle. Not our country. Not our business. Let's just enjoy our drinks and watch from a safe distance."

"But it's interesting," said the curious. "We should be seeing what's going on and get involved. It's history in the making."

"We must show our support," claimed the committed. "We have lived here a long time and we are part of Hong Kong too. These are our friends, our work colleagues and our team mates out there."

"But this is a Chinese issue," countered the diffident. "It would be hypocritical to pretend we are part of it. We may all get thrown out in a few months if things turn nasty! And we are all out of here in '97 anyway!"

"We can't just sit back indifferently. We can show our support and solidarity. It's important that expats and foreigners and the international community speak up for the Hong Kong people," countered the engaged.

In the end half a dozen of us self-consciously wandered over into the thickening crowd to taste the atmosphere. It was vastly different from the previous mass meeting I had attended. It was consciously political, with thundering condemnations of the Chinese government from the stage, declarations for democracy in Hong Kong and demands that the British government act to protect the people with representative safeguards and the issuing of British passports. This was passion politics from the gut, such as had never been seen in Hong Kong. This was determined, not hysterical – the crowd was emotional, but controlled and resolute.

Instead of hostility or questioning about our presence, people came to us and thanked us for showing up. They nodded approval. Some came and shook our hands.

"You must tell your government," they urged us. "Tell your friends what's happening here. Tell the British government not to abandon us. Tell the world not to let Hong Kong fall into the hands of the murdering Chinese government."

We stayed for about an hour, listening to speakers such as barrister Martin Lee, one of the best known Democratic leaders, his voice quavering with feeling. Emily Lau, ex-journalist, more radical, demanding the British act with a safe route out for Hong Kong residents, and others, the firebrands, stoking up the crowd.

\Nothing got out of hand, but this mass solidarity, rallying around a political idea, was a new phenomenon in Hong Kong. Politically indifferent, materialistic Hong Kong had found its voice.

As the weeks and months passed, the situation stabilised, albeit in repressive fashion, in China. In Hong Kong the new political awareness that seized the Hong Kong people began to take an organised shape. For most Hong Kong passport holders, the key question was how to acquire insurance – a safety net in case the coming handover to China in 1997 went badly wrong.

Some demanded the British Government grant all six million British passports, and if necessary, like the Ugandan Asians, receive them into the UK, but this was always a difficult choice to sell to the UK electorate at a time when immigration was a sensitive issue.

A few – those closest to the colonial government – gained that option. Others sought US, Australian, Canadian or Singaporean passports, and some succeeded. The aim was not necessarily to go to these destinations, but to have the fallback position should the future look black.

Meanwhile, the British Government sought ways to support the territory. The first was a financial gesture – investing (Hong Kong money) massively in the new international airport at Chek Lap Kok, to demonstrate continued belief in the future. Initially, it backfired, as the Chinese Government took exception to this defiance and declared the project a white elephant which they would not recognise after 1997. The impasse led to the recall of British Governor Wilson, who was replaced by ex-Tory Party Chairman Chris Patten.

Patten, an experienced politician rather than a foreign office civil servant like previous governors, set about introducing a measure of democracy to Hong Kong's Legislative Council. It was seen by some as a cynical move to enable Britain to depart the colony with a measure of self-respect, rather than abandoning the residents.

Vitriolic opposition spewed from Beijing. Labelling Patten a whore and calling him "Fat Pang" the official Chinese sources excoriated Patten at every turn. Sinophile foreign office mandarins undermined him, arguing that this last ditch democratisation was pointless and merely jeopardising the handover agreement with a major trading partner.

Local business tycoons, expat and Chinese, were concerned that bad relations with Beijing would harm business. Why, they asked, would Britain want to introduce democracy seven years before the handover, when for the previous century and a half it hadn't even been considered? Hong Kong people, the argument ran, were inherently apolitical. They were in Hong Kong to make money, to run their businesses and to build a better life for their families.

Both sides of this criticism missed the point. The real driver for Britain's change of heart was certainly related to the potential loss of international reputation should the UK just walk out on its responsibilities. But underlying that was the great upsurge in demand for representation from the Hong Kong people themselves, for whom the Tiananmen Square massacre was a traumatic moment. At least, with a degree of representation, they had a slight chance of defending themselves against any further Chinese Government acts of tyranny.

As an expatriate experiencing those tense and emotional months, there was nothing I could really contribute. However, it did strengthen my emotional ties with Hong Kong and increase my admiration for its down-to-earth, irreverent and resilient people.

As I write this, many years later, I look at a framed photograph hung on the study wall. Another famous scene of that time, it portrays a long view from a hotel balcony towards Tiananmen Square. Where a few days before had been thousands of tented protesters, were then rows of People's Army tanks. In a foreground on an access road, a long column of tanks is making its way out of the Square. But they are stalled, for in front of the leading tank is a tiny solitary figure, blocking its way. You can make out he is wearing a white shirt and carrying what looks like a bag of shopping in each hand. The leading tank has swerved to avoid him, but he has clearly stepped to the side to continue his defiance. No one ever found out who this individual was, or what happened to him.

Horse Shampoo

I never planned a career in public relations. Like many things in life it developed opportunistically. In fact, in my days as a schoolteacher I would have adopted a morally superior position, looking down on an occupation which seemed to hover between journalism, business and entertainment, without requiring the talent or looks required by any of those three.

But then I was a prig in those days and PR was eventually to provide me with a varied, amusing, and unpredictable career with reasonable financial rewards. At first, on leaving my teaching job in Hong Kong in 1981 at the age of 31, I had ambitions to be a freelance journalist and writer, living a bohemian existence from the outpourings of my typewriter. This dream was based on some modest success I had enjoyed writing book reviews for the Far Eastern Economic Review, a few articles for airline magazines and the North Herts Express. Armed with this limited portfolio and plenty of imagination I aimed to thrust my way into the Hong Kong media scene.

Six months later I was writing press releases about show jumping, boat shows and cycling races, having learnt the age-old lesson that "artists" don't necessarily earn enough to pay the rent. Having been referred to a go-ahead young PR company, run by an ambitious and creative Londoner, Jeff Mann, I discovered the value of a steady income and an enjoyable and challenging job.

Public relations in Hong Kong in those days was in the early stage of development. It was dominated by a few major international companies, such as Hill and Knowlton, Burson Marsteller and Edelman, which, together, dominated the large corporate, multi-national scene. However, Hong Kong's spectacular economic growth and increasing business sophistication, in the wake of the opening up of China, meant that a broad-based domestic and international client base was developing fast, with international companies looking to Hong Kong as a base for penetration into China and other Asian markets.

On the media side a lively but limited and undemanding press and broadcast offering meant that publicity channels were relatively easy to access for PR professionals. There were only two English language dailies – the South China Morning Post and the Hong Kong Standard – along with a dozen or so worthwhile Chinese papers and two TV channels. In this encouraging context of the 80s, a crop of home-grown companies, who knew the local market well, were emerging. Jeff's company, Jeff Mann and Associates, or JMA, was among them and Jeff astutely cornered an emerging new area – sports PR.

I found myself working in a fast-moving, dynamic young company, initially with some six or eight staff, but expanding week by week. Compared to the orderly, responsible world of teaching, PR agency work, catering to a range of clients and projects, juggling tasks and priorities, was chaotic and exhilarating. After the moral burdens of teaching, and the routines of lesson preparation and marking, it was a relief. Colleagues were young – at thirty-one I was for a while the oldest – mostly single and a mix of Chinese and European. At first I focused on producing press releases and other editorial, managing a small team of writers and translators.

Making the transition from formal academic and educational writing to commercial copywriting wasn't difficult, though needed more practice than I thought. Soon I was concentrating on the sports work, which I enjoyed, having always been active in sports myself.

JMA had been instrumental in establishing the highly successful Hong Kong Rugby Sevens, working with the major sponsors – the Hong Kong Shanghai Bank and Cathay Pacific Airways. This rugby tournament was a weekend-long, drink-fuelled but good-humoured fiesta for Hong Kong's expats and thousands of visitors. In addition, JMA helped set up the Hong Kong Golf Open and the Hong Kong Squash Open, bringing in major sponsors, whose object of course, was to raise popular awareness of their brands through international media exposure.

After a year or so I took over running the management of these major events, sitting on the organising committees, implementing the promotional strategies and acting as press officer during the events themselves. It was a steep learning curve, and on events weekends, demanding and exhausting. Working on sports events meant too little sleep, too much alcohol – the press had to be entertained! – and living on adrenalin.

Being a keen sportsman I relished meeting the celebrity players and helping organise their media appearances. Few were prima donnas. I also appreciated the company of journalists and helping them get the necessary material – results, comment, facts and figures – to tight deadlines, gave a feeling of importance! Our press team at the Sevens had to look after over 300 journalists from around the world.

As well as these spectacular events, JMA lived off a number of retainer clients, the most lucrative of which were Marlboro and Carlsberg. The fact that these products engaged in healthy sport to promote themselves was entirely artful. Marlboro, the flagship brand of Philip Morris, was the best selling cigarette in Hong Kong and a major international sales success.

At that time, in the 1980s, many people, including myself, smoked and the full story of the link between smoking and lung disease was not widely known. The Philip Morris people were fully aware of the effect of linking Marlboro with a healthy lifestyle, giving the brand, along with its cowboy image of rugged independence (i.e. I'll smoke if I want to) the values of an active outdoor life (i.e. smoking is healthy).

In tune with this marketing strategy, Marlboro sponsored a range of sports – but not those anaerobic activities that required deep breathing! Horse racing, cycling, wind surfing, show jumping and motor racing all carried the Marlboro logo. None of us worried about the hypocrisy of this in those days. The sports associations receiving Marlboro funding and professional organising support, certainly benefited and developed with this backing.

Motor racing in particular suited the Marlboro profile – macho, risky and glamorous, and the main event of the year for them was the Macau Grand Prix. This was a Formula Three version of Monaco's famous race. Like Monaco, Macau offered a tight, twisting city course, which prevented much overtaking but resulted in highly entertaining and dangerous tactics. There were frequent crashes and controversies. For four days the casino city of Macau was one huge party. For us PR staff it was once again early starts and late nights. I was never seduced by the motor racing itself, but the event was certainly high octane action and socialising.

Marlboro logos were plastered on the cars and Marlboro signage dominated the track. I was surprised by the obsessive accuracy with which the Marlboro marketing boys mapped the TV cameras' positioning and angles to choose the siting for their trackside signage. It captured every possible moment of TV coverage. Whatever part of the race you were watching on TV you were also seeing the Marlboro brand!

Through Marlboro motor racing I met Formula One world champion Alain Prost, who came to Hong Kong for a short promotional visit. My job involved meeting him and organising a media welcome at the airport, arranging a few select interviews and managing a mass photo signing opportunity for fans outside the Peninsula Hotel. This place was Hong Kong's most luxurious hotel, where he was staying.

From the start the project was problematic. First, the arrival at the airport was a shambles, because hundreds of fans swamped the hall to catch a glimpse of their Gallic hero and instead of an orderly press interview we found ourselves manhandling Prost through a frenzied mob. Our media programme was also difficult because Prost was more miserable than the most misanthropic Parisian waiter. Grumpy and monosyllabic, he was unco-operative and unsmiling.

Then the photo signing at the front of the Peninsula also degenerated into farce. We had Prost seated behind a table with a pile of his photos, which he was supposed to sign individually for his adoring fans. Unfortunately our publicity proved too successful and hundreds of fans showed up. They crowded around the table as soon as Prost appeared, jostling and pushing to get to him. The signed photos ran out in minutes. Meanwhile, the general melee was attracting even more curious onlookers and then the police turned up.

By this time I was sitting under the table, hidden by the table cloth, frantically forging Prost's signature onto as many blank photos as I could and passing them up to him to give out. To this day I have no doubt many a proud Hong Kong racing fan is showing his friends his personally signed photo of Prost, unaware it is a poor facsimile of the real thing dashed off by yours truly.

I met several world champions at this time, and most were more agreeable than Monsieur Misery. It fell upon me, for example, to host for a Chinese meal one evening the world darts champion Eric Bristow. He was accompanied by his partner Maureen Flowers, who was the ladies darts world champion. Eric, famously known as the "Crafty Cockney" was easy going and affable. I remember being staggered at the thought he practised six hours a day. Obviously such monotonous repetition worked, for Bristow dominated the sport for some years.

Two more world champions I hosted were related. Jahangir Khan, at the end of long reign at the top of squash, came to play in the Hong Kong Open before retiring. He was then succeeded in this title by his nephew Jansher Khan. Whilst the uncle was amenable and outgoing, his heir proved a cold fish. But Jansher was an extraordinary squash player, with abnormal endurance that wore down his opponents. In his first Hong Kong Open final, he outlasted his challenger in the very first rally, by keeping the ball alive for no less than 17 minutes.

On another occasion, JMA provided the PR for a special football tournament, sponsored and arranged by the Danish beer giant Carlsberg, who had a very successful brewery in Hong Kong. They invited the Danish champions, Brondby, to take part, and I found myself hosting a Chinese banquet for them. Next to me sat a very shy, huge young man, who was Brondby's goalkeeper. At 18 years old he was tipped for great things, though his company was far from stimulating that night! The reserved, inarticulate giant was Peter Schmeichel, who went on to achieve world fame as Manchester United's and Denmark's star goal minder.

These encounters, and the hectic social life revolving around events, corporate clients, sportsmen and journalists were stimulating, but after five years, I grew weary of the anti-social hours and heavy drinking culture. It was time to think about career development, and at the age of 36, I moved on.

So, having applied for, and been offered, a post at the Hong Kong Trade Development Council, I left Jeff Mann and the team on good terms, and focused my newly acquired PR skills on another area – trade and investment promotion.

The HKTDC, as it was commonly known, was a global organisation, with over 600 staff spanning 15 offices around the world. It was well funded, taking its income from a percentage of Hong Kong's export earnings, which had soared during the 80's as China opened up.

Taking on the role of international press manager, I oversaw a small team of three writers in producing the publicity material for the overseas offices. In addition, we handled the media relations for a busy annual programme of trade fairs in Hong Kong as well as overseas promotions. We looked after visiting press, and were the "English language" department preparing speeches for senior staff and other promotional material.

It seemed like the perfect job for me. Making use of the economics and history background I brought with me from teaching, it involved some creative writing, dealing face-to-face with journalists, and interesting travel. There was, however, a major obstacle to my enjoying the role – the boss! Chief Executive Jack So was the most disagreeable person I ever worked for. Extremely clever and sharp tongued, he seemed to delight in making life difficult for his staff. Unfortunately, in the first couple of years of my time at the HKTDC I had to deal directly with him.

I also attempted to write speeches for him but nothing was good enough. I suggested at an early stage that it would be helpful and productive if he briefed me on his intentions with a particular speech before I started writing. This was met with the brusque query that what did I think I was employed for. As a result he would return my drafts, which I had worked on for many hours, with noted comments such as "This is rubbish, do it again!", but with no other clue as to what was actually wrong with them.

His management technique of hostile confrontation left most of us baffled and demoralised and therefore proved counterproductive. For my first year there I was unhappy and searched for alternatives, but after a new manager arrived to supervise me and therefore intervene between me and Mr So, matters improved and I was able to gain some reward from the job.

Running the press office for the HKTDC's trade fairs was one aspect I enjoyed. In tune with Hong Kong's remarkable economic resurgence, as China opened up to the world, the organisation ran a growing number of international trade fairs at the brand new Hong Kong Convention and Exhibition Centre. These fairs covered sectors such as Fashion, Leather goods, Toys, Household products and many other categories.

I found myself, bizarrely, hosting top fashion writers from around the world, from publications like the New York Times, Cosmopolitan, the Frankfurter Zeitung, and top Japanese papers. Being the least fashionable candidate for this glamorous role, this didn't come naturally, but it was highly entertaining, and a valuable publicity role for Hong Kong at a time when style rather than low price was becoming central to the territory's success.

In addition, I worked closely with the HKTDC's chair Lydia Dunn. This elegant and energetic Chinese woman, who was dubbed the "Iron Lady of Asia" worked tirelessly for Hong Kong's benefit. Writing speeches for her was demanding – she was a perfectionist – but she was supportive in the process and I found the work politically fascinating and personally absorbing. At this time in the late eighties, as Hong Kong's future status was being robustly debated between the UK and China, she had to tread a delicate line between the two powers in defending the interests of the six million people of Hong Kong.

As the face of Hong Kong in its international promotional efforts to position itself as a modern managerial and financial centre, she also travelled the world. I accompanied her with delegations as press officer, setting up media engagements, briefing her and generally "handholding" her through busy days of appointments with press, officials and politicians.

For me it was quite nerve-wracking but thrilling to be sitting with this sparrow-like but powerful woman in a limousine, travelling through the streets of Tokyo and briefing her. "Right Frank," she would say, as we dashed from one meeting to the next, "Let's run through the talk notes for the next meeting," with the Japanese minister for trade or whoever was next on the agenda. Our schedules would run from breakfast time to midnight. I was exhausted but she would remain composed and immaculately presented throughout.

Our greatest test came with the Tiananmen Square massacre in 1989. The revulsion against the Chinese government's action fundamentally changed attitudes in Hong Kong, where it produced wide-spread fear, and the whole dynamic of the negotiations about the future. But in the short run it also placed Hong Kong's economic being in doubt. For several weeks the HKTDC was bombarded with calls from around the world enquiring about Hong Kong's trading status. We had to reassure everyone that it was business as usual, and trade was continuing, but there was a real fear of civil war in China and a complete collapse of investor confidence in Hong Kong. Capital could have flown out in an instant given Hong Kong's lack of restriction on money movement.

Very challenging and sometimes disagreeable though it was, the role at the HKTDC gave me renewed confidence and toughened me up. I travelled to new places, including Vancouver, Seattle, Stockholm, Munich, Berlin, Paris, Tokyo, Nagoya and Beijing and met leading politicians, business people and journalists on a daily basis.

By 1990 my situation had changed. I had married and had a child. I had to plan ahead and the HKTDC didn't seem to offer a path forward. Given the organisation was localising, quite rightly, the opportunities for expats were diminishing. Taking the bold option, I resigned with the aim of using my new-found status to obtain a corporate PR position. Fortunately, my wife had an income to sustain us while I attempted it.

Matters took a different course from that planned. I failed to get the high-level corporate role I expected my HKTDC reputation to win me. Despite a couple of promising interviews, people didn't have the high opinion of my capabilities as I did.

Consequently, I fell back on freelancing, working from home. I wrote speeches, corporate brochures, company strategies and advertisements – anything for which I was paid. Within a few months I was earning more than I had at the HKTDC, and took the next logical step of incorporating myself. Within six months, Wingate PR was born.

Another unplanned twist in life therefore turned me into an entrepreneur. I really hadn't a clue about running a business, but financial need is the mother of invention and somehow I bluffed my way along. I recruited staff as business grew – a secretary first, then a Chinese language assistant. Then another Chinese second-in-command. Then an English language number two.

At first we won projects, but, like all PR agencies, our aim was to gain clients paying a monthly retainer on an annual contract basis, to provide the financial certainty to plan ahead. Within two years we had a reasonable portfolio of brand name retainers, notably the Hong Kong Tourist Association, Mobil Oil, Kodak, and Ericsson, the Swedish mobile phone company.

The routine mixed with the strange. One of my regular ad hoc clients was the corporate affairs director of a very well-known Chinese tycoon, or rather, the son of the tycoon. He demanded major speeches within 24 hours and my client would always call me in a panic. "The little monster," he would whine, "needs something for tomorrow night!" I would dash over and together we would cobble together a briefing. I would then work through the night to deliver a draft by the next morning. During the day we re-worked it several times as the little monster rejected various drafts. This was exhausting, but very lucrative, as, money was no object.

Ericsson proved to be our anchor client. I had a good working relationship with the no-nonsense New Zealander who ran the company. During the nineties the Swedish mobile system maker made the headway in Hong Kong and China with its mobile phones and was by far the leading brand. They anticipated the smaller handset and the onset of 3G with its potential for mobile internet.

However, the good burgers of Sweden, who ran Ericsson, were slow to recognise the growing value of handsets as accessories. While they produced simple, solid, boring phones, with excellent technology, rivals such as Nokia and Samsung were producing coloured phones of all sizes and shapes to suit all age groups and moods. By the end of the decade Ericsson had lost out to the competition. Nevertheless, their patronage sustained my small PR outfit.

If Ericsson was the bread and butter client, "Mane and Tail" Shampoo was the most bizarre. I met the garrulous, charming and eccentric lady who intended to sell this product in Hong Kong at a trade fair and she employed us to introduce it to the territory. The shampoo had been developed, unsurprisingly, for horse hair, but in the US had also proved a hit with the owners, whose hair, apparently, benefited from whatever strong concoction went into it.

It was always going to be a long shot in Hong Kong, where horses were either for betting on or possibly eating. Somehow the cultural gap proved too great. We attempted a press conference – doing our very best to convince a sceptical media that this was a breakthrough in hair care. Our American client arranged for three leading Hong Kong hairdressers to come.

Half a dozen journalists did show up, but our host did not. We all waited 45 minutes, by which time all but one Chinese hack and one hairdresser remained. When she finally flounced in, she declared she had had to spend sufficient time in preparing her own hair. Undeterred by the paucity of audience, she then delivered a 30-minute lecture to the empty room. Afterwards she fired us for failing to deliver enough publicity, but she did pay most of the bill. And so it was that "Mane and Tail" fell at the first fence.

At another press conference we organised for the Dutch Trade Commission, whose national trade minister was visiting, the problem turned out to be too many press showing up. Unfortunately for us, a good number of them were impostors, posing as journalists. They were members of Greenpeace and were there to disrupt the conference, thereby creating as much publicity as possible for their own cause.

The obscure issue motivating them concerned the Dutch selling decommissioned ships to China for breakage. Apparently, they often contained asbestos and this could harm the workers and damage the environment. The Dutch refuted the facts of the case but didn't deter the Greenpeace Crusaders, who rushed to the head table, leapt upon it and unfurled a huge banner, much to the delight of the photographers present.

I tried to intervene, grabbing one of the interlopers by the knees to remove them from the table. Unfortunately, this protester was an attractive Chinese lady, and when my photo appeared in the dailies the next day I looked like a pervert clutching her legs with an embarrassed grin on my face.

Despite these hiccups, Wingate PR gently prospered. We grew to ten staff and in 1996 a London-based PR company, looking to build an Asian division, bought us out. This arrangement gave me a four-year term to continue managing the company, with the objective of expanding to Beijing and Singapore.

This proved an ambition too far, partly because we had little capital to invest but were trying to grow organically, creating the income to fund the expansion as we proceeded. But more damaging was the Asian financial crisis, which enveloped the region in 1998 and abruptly reduced business prospects in our new offices. We had to admit defeat.

Nevertheless, the final two years of my PR life in Hong Kong, before the family decamped to London, were successful, largely on account of the dotcom boom. Young entrepreneurs with grand but unrealised visions for the internet were throwing money at publicity, and agencies like us were happy to oblige.

One young American with the unforgettable name of Nimrod Winkelstein wanted us to arrange a press conference to promote his new online business relating to hotel bookings.

This website was still at concept stage and hadn't even been designed. "It'll cost 20,000 Hong Kong dollars," I suggested optimistically. "No, no," he replied, "You need to spend at least 50,000!" The point was, he explained, that his investors expected him to maintain a certain "burn rate" of marketing spend to assure them he would be first to the market with his ideas. This was not untypical of that period of web mania.

Along with our less spectacular but sound clientele, these projects enabled the company to make money, and I was able to leave a profitable balance sheet at the end of 2000, when we finally departed Hong Kong for London.

My twenty years in public relations in Hong Kong had been unexpected, unpredictable and stimulating. It was an adventure, during which I met many impressive people, many delusional upstarts and the inevitable charlatans. I often reflect on the fact that such an adventure wouldn't have happened if I had stayed in London.

Photo Section

First impressions – flying in precariously to Hong Kong's old Kai Tak Airport, skimming over the rooftops of Mongkok

Hello concrete jungle

Squatter huts of the 1970s

Colourful Hong Kong streets

My first Hong Kong class – at St. Paul's Boys School – who nicknamed me "Poxy Chicken"

Sporting glory at Hong Kong Stadium (bearded author far right)

Daughter Sophie samples Cantonese food stall

Hong Kong night life – legendary Red Lips bar centre

Author (second right) trying to shield world motor racing
champion, Alain Prost, on behalf of clients Marlboro

Only expat hosting joyful Japanese trade delegation

Sharing a joke with Asia's "Iron Lady" Lydia (later Baroness) Dunn

Promoting "Mane 'n' Tail" shampoo (unsuccessfully)

Lunch in most famous Chiu Chow restaurant, before the
"Chopper Incident"

With our delightful Philippina home help Marjorie and daughter
Sophie

My dear Hong Kong friends, Woo and wife Helen, with my wife,
Uschi, and Sophie

Early shot of new China Bank Tower, symbol of approaching
Chinese resumption of sovereignty

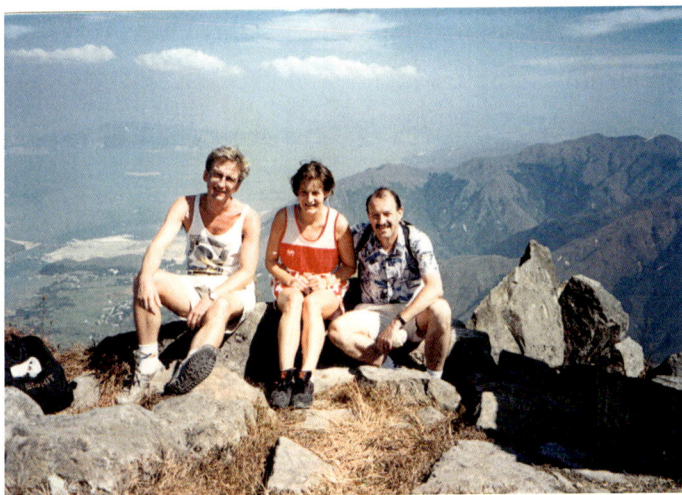

On top of Hong Kong. Conquering Lantau Peak with Uschi and friend Werner

Chinese Chopper

Having moved into my first home in Hong Kong, in a block of flats in which I was the only non-Chinese, initial impressions included unfamiliar household noises. There was, of course, the sound overheard of snatches of family rows and shouts in Cantonese; the alien tones of classical Cantonese opera from open windows; and the ubiquitous clattering of mahjong tiles.

The Hong Kong Chinese were addicted to this cross between bridge and dominoes and often played it late into the night. The repetitive clacking of the porcelain tiles during the course of the game and then the rhythmic scraping as the tiles were mixed on the table top for the next round ("dry swimming" the Cantonese called it -- the movement of the hands resembling the breast stroke) soon became familiar and bearable.

One noise, however, puzzled and irritated me for some time. This was a frequent tapping noise, usually in the evening, which seemed to come from several directions at once. It would last for some minutes, stop, then start again. For the first week or two I had no idea of the source of this intrusive noise, and, once or twice, I banged on my ceiling with a broomstick in a vain attempt to alert my neighbours that they were disturbing me. It was pointless and ignorant of me, for I was soon enlightened by a visiting Chinese friend that the tapping was no more sinister than the sound of a Chinese chopper in action on the chopping board, preparing various ingredients for the evening meal.

The chopper is the essential tool in Chinese cuisine, along with the wok. In skilful hands it can perform the full array of cutting tasks needed to prepare the bite-sized food ready for cooking Chinese dishes. A Chinese chef can wield the heavy sharp implement with delicate finesse, as in slicing a clove of garlic into wafer thin slices or peeling an orange. It can also be swung with vigour, as when dismembering a chicken or even a pig.

It is remarkably flexible and deft, when used by trained operators. Equally, it is a legendary weapon of fearsome reputation. Traditionally a choice of the dreaded triads – the Chinese mafia – it is swift, silent and lethal. We occasionally read with horror in the local media about triad retribution crimes, where the victim, usually a "grass" or a rival gang member, would be crippled for life by having their hamstrings severed.

This kind of blood-curdling story was, however, far from my mind in July, 1990, when my wife and I planned an adventurous long weekend trip to Mainland China. On the contrary, life was bright and positive. We were newly married, my wife was pregnant, and I had just started my own business.

China was opening up. Since Deng Xiaoping had launched the Open Door policy in 1979, economic growth and change had been spectacular in China. As part of that policy, which liberalised the Chinese economy, freeing it from the austere and at times fatal Maoist centralism, Deng had established a number of Special Economic Zones, mostly on the coast. They were designed to attract foreign investment, stimulate trade with the outside world, and pioneer more free market practices. One such zone was Shenzhen, adjacent to Hong Kong and another, further up the coast of Guangdong Province, was Shantou.

Shantou was our target for that weekend's trip, for no better reason than it was within range and still seemed to be "real" Mainland China. It was also within a day trip of Chiu Chow, a town and area reputed for its cuisine and historical sites. We could experience communist China before it was swept away in economic growth and reform, before "the socialist market with Chinese characteristics" changed the face of our vast neighbour for ever with its tsunami of consumerism and materialism.

We decided to go by local passenger boat – a regular ferry that plied the Chinese coast, picking up and dropping its human cargo at the ports of Guangdong, Fujian and Zhenjiang Provinces. Our intrepid gang comprised us two, with nine-year-old son, German friends Kurt and Barbara, Kurt's Cantonese girlfriend Molly Fung and Robert our Austrian art teacher friend.

The German connection was strong, as my wife was from Bonn, and I had taught for several years in the English stream of the German International School in Hong Kong. Like many Germans, imbued with "wanderlust" they were hardened travellers and preferred to shun luxury in the pursuit of genuine experience. My wife, for one, had hitchhiked around China on her own several years previously. So I felt reasonably well protected by this intrepid teutonic squad.

Our chosen mode of conveyance proved to be quite a test in its own right. The rust bucket of a passenger ferry we boarded that evening could well have been a survivor of World War Two. It was uncomfortably overcrowded and stank of diesel fuel and garlic. I noticed we were the only non-Chinese to hazard the journey that weekend. The idea was that we would book cabins and get a good sleep overnight on the voyage. However, it immediately became apparent that this comfortable notion was out of step with reality.

The cabins, with walls of cast iron, were unbearably hot. This was mid-summer in the South China Sea. Daytime temperatures of 33 degrees centigrade were the norm. The

115

metal walls of the cabin were almost too hot to touch, and the small porthole, which only had a diameter of six inches anyway, was rusted solidly shut. There was no air-conditioning on this tub, no fans, no fresh air and no breeze.

We had little choice but to join the other passengers on the deck in the open air. Even this didn't prove easy, as we had difficulty in finding enough space for our gang to sit on the deck together. And so we began a long, stiflingly hot, uncomfortable night. Luckily we managed to buy some bottled water and beer and this helped sustain our spirits as the dark hours went by.

By the time we finally reached Shantou the next morning, and first light appeared on the horizon at about six o'clock, we were tired, thirsty, hungry and sore from sitting on the hard metal deck. It was a relief when the sun came up and our antiquated ferry swung clumsily against the huge wooden pillars of the public quay in Shantou and shuddered to a stop. It was just after five and we looked forward to the comfort of the hotel, a hot shower and a nap before embarking on the exploration of Deng's new China.

China was nothing if not a test of patience. Instead of piling off the ferry, we were informed proudly that we had arrived two hours early. Unfortunately this only meant more torture as we endured the rapidly increasing temperature and humidity on a packed deck, until Chinese immigration officials, dressed in the baggy, shapeless green uniforms of the army, ambled along the quayside and finally allowed us to disembark.

We poured off with the travelling masses, eager to stretch our legs and investigate the new economic zone. But our enthusiasm was then dampened further by an hour and a half's queue in immigration, shuffling exhausted past curious but sullen guards. Finally, we were cleared by an equally humourless and pedantic immigration officer, who clearly considered customer relations a capitalist aberration.

At last we stepped out of the immigration area, which was also a major railway station, hoping to find a taxi or bus to take us to our pre-booked hotel. But outside we were aghast to find ourselves in a great ocean of people, mostly sitting or lying around, with piles of luggage, almost all packed in the bulky striped blue and red plastic bags favoured by the Chinese at that time.

It was no exaggeration to say there were many thousands, lounging on an area at least the size of a football pitch. Of course, it was a holiday time, and migrant workers, the new Chinese proletariat, were on the move – back to the countryside to see their families. It was disquieting. No-one disturbed or harried us, or begged from us. But it seemed everyone regarded us with mistrust and suspicion. It appeared there were as yet no smiles but many stares for foreign tourists in the newly opened China.

With a sense of relief, our weary troop arrived at Shantou's newest hotel half an hour later. We had been spotted in the mass by taxi drivers as profitable fares and delivered without fuss.

The staff at the hotel were obliging, deferential, charming, shy and amateurish. The manager, however, was sharp and friendly, as well as a fluent English speaker. He snapped out his orders officiously, showing off his authority, as we were conveyed to our rooms with great ceremony. You would find him successful in any type of economic structure. He would certainly flourish in the new age – he stood out like an ambitious cadre.

Although clearly only a few years old, the hotel was already shabby and poorly maintained. There were many cigarette stains on the carpet and the malfunctioning toilet didn't flush properly. We noticed the uniforms of the staff were grubby, with stains on the shiny lapels of their jackets. We were also quite disconcerted by the appearance of an entirely self-confident mouse, which popped up on top of the TV set, as we watched it, to munch contentedly on one of the biscuits from a packet left there. It took some chasing away.

Nevertheless, we accepted all this stoically. After all, this was a China adventure and ten years ago such a hotel wouldn't have even existed. Above all the staff were very well-meaning, extremely helpful and friendly. Thus began our China trip, and the next day we set off for the nearby historic town of Chiu Chow.

Chiu Chow was well known in Hong Kong, because the latter had proved a refuge to many from the area fleeing Mao's Red Army in 1948/49. The Chiu Chow community was an established feature of Hong Kong, not least because a number of notable Chinese tycoons came from that town, famous for its entrepreneurial vigour. Li Ka Shing, arguably the most successful and mega-rich of them all, originated from a humble Chiu Chow background.

But the place also had its own dialect, similar to Cantonese, as well as its own cuisine. Lightly flavoured, fresh and famously healthy Chiu Chow favourites include duck and goose as well as offal dishes. Being culinary adventurers, this attracted us, so we made for what the guide books told us was Chiu Chow's most famous restaurant.

Here we were treated as VIPs. The food was exemplary, but the experience was bizarre. When we arrived at lunchtime, the place was deserted. The sleepy and diffident looking staff, on recognising Western customers, suddenly leapt into action with beaming smiles. Their first job, before we could even sit down, was to sweep up. This was because the entire floor of the whole restaurant was covered in a thick carpet of discarded tissues, paper napkins, cigarette packets and butts.

Thoughtfully the staff cleared away the debris from the prime table in the best situated place – the corner window table. They swept clean a perfect circle, about a yard greater in circumference than the round table itself. Here we settled ourselves, slightly alarmed at the chickens above us. Not live chickens but ready to cook chickens, which were apparently being dried by being suspended from the large fan directly above our table. So as we ate, the three chickens circled around above us.

The other aspect of Chiu Chow's most recommended restaurant that surprised us was the old lady with the wide but toothless smile who crouched in the single toilet washing dishes in a plastic bowl. Unabashed, she was warm in her greeting and chatted non-stop in Chinese while we carried out our personal functions.

But the eccentricities aside, the food was outstanding. Suitably nourished we set out into the teeming rain and high humidity to explore Chiu Chow's historic delights.

Most memorable was the Kaiyun temple – a Buddhist centre, which had somehow escaped the ravages and mindless vandalism of the cultural revolution.

It was neglected, overgrown with weeds and creepers, yet retained an eerie sanctity. The elaborately carved pillars and wall decorations were battered by time, but represented a link with ancient China which was all too rare after the orgy of violence initiated by Mao swept away so much of beauty and historical value.

Back in Shantou, that same evening, tired and damp, we decided we didn't want to go far, but to eat near the hotel, somewhere local preferably, and off the tourist track. Our search was brief, for we found a basic street stall, or dai pai dong as the Cantonese call them, almost opposite the hotel where we stayed. It was rough and ready, but interesting, with some unrecognisable seafood dishes on display on the simple trestle table, along with some favourites we were well acquainted with. The place looked like a large garage or workshop, with bare concrete walls and uneven floors, wooden tables and plastic chairs.

The staff at the food stall were all smiles and very hospitable, clearly pleased to have foreign guests and keen to show off their dishes. Six of us sat down initially at the rough tables and Molly, being the Mandarin speaker – as well as her native Cantonese – started ordering a few dishes and we were soon tucking into prawns, rice, fish and other delicacies.

After a while though we noticed that more and more dishes were arriving at our table. We asked Molly what exactly she had ordered, for there seemed to be far too much. On enquiring with the waiters, she was told that we were welcome to try these extra dishes, implying we could then order them if we liked them. We also noticed a growing crowd of curious spectators gathering at the open road side of the food stall, obviously keen to see how the foreigners – "waiguoren" – were coping with the local cuisine.

While enjoying the food, we were becoming uncomfortable, because far too many dishes were appearing, which we had not ordered, and didn't want, and the crowd of spectators was increasing, blocking the whole entrance side. Time to go we decided, and asked for the bill. This is when the trouble began.

The smiling host, clearly very pleased with himself, presented us with a handwritten bill for eight hundred renminbi. We couldn't believe it. There must be a mistake! Eight hundred renminbi was equivalent then to the same amount of Hong Kong dollars, or about seventy pounds. This was the kind of price you might pay on a luxury night out at one of Hong Kong's most prestigious Chinese restaurants or international hotels. It was equivalent to about a year's salary in China. For a food stall like this, even in Hong Kong, which was ten times more expensive, you would expect to pay, at maximum, thirty or forty Hong Kong dollars.

Molly politely pointed out that there must be a mistake and asked for clarification. The smile on the stall owner's face was replaced with an angry scowl. No, there was no mistake – we had taken many of his finest dishes and now we must pay up. The atmosphere rapidly turned sour.

Clearly it would be ridiculous to pay such an amount. We didn't even have that much cash on us. The four of us – Kurt, Robert, Molly and myself – decided we shouldn't pay and we refused the bill. Using the limited Mandarin I knew, I said it was too much. We would pay a reasonable amount. Then the situation became really ugly and the Chinese choppers first appeared. The stall owner and three of his staff now stood in front of our table, each holding a large cleaver in a threatening way and preventing us from leaving. The crowd of onlookers behind them had swollen into a large crowd, evidently fascinated by the prospect of a confrontation involving waiguoren.

The stall owner began shouting angrily and Molly, at whom the diatribe was directed, began to cry. Kurt, tall, athletic and now offended, stood up to challenge the bullies and defend his girl. I dragged him back quickly into his seat. This was no time for heroics. At this point, my pregnant wife, taking advantage of the distraction, slipped away with Robert. They pushed their way through the rapidly growing throng, now filling the open side, and headed for the hotel.

What were we to do? I repeated the word jingfang – police – several times, gesticulating that they should call one, but this only served to agitate our aggressive hosts even more. The choppers were being waved around and one was then without warning thudded into the table in front of us.

The blood drained from my face. We were all shocked and frightened. We just sat still, unsure what to do, while the crowd seemed highly entertained by the whole scene. I recall the sea of Chinese faces, jostling to get a view of us, grinning, laughing and commentating on the action. The stall owner was now raging at us in a paroxysm of fury.

And then, quite suddenly, just as our fear reached a peak, and as if someone had waved a magic wand, the crowd parted and melted away. Our antagonists scuttled like cockroaches into the shadows. In marched the young manager from our hotel across the road, with two policemen behind him and my wife and Robert following them.

"Come with me please," he said calmly in modulated English, "Don't worry! We will handle this." It was an invitation accepted without a moment's hesitation.

Some hours later, at about 10 o'clock, when we were about to go to bed, there was a knock on our hotel door. We had by then fully recovered from our ordeal, discussed it at length and decided we were warriors for justice and fair restaurant prices throughout the world.

It was the manager who had saved us from potential mutilation. He was accompanied by two policemen who, he explained, wished to take us to the police station to investigate our case. Molly – for obvious language reasons – Kurt and myself dutifully followed the policemen on foot to the local station, some ten minutes walk away.

We were shown into a crumbling, shabby, and gloomy building, where we were invited to sit in a bare cell-like room lit by dim, unshaded light bulbs hanging from the ceiling. We three sat on a wooden bench along one wall. On the wet and uneven bare concrete floor, spread before us, were numerous dishes of food – some of them half finished, apparently the ones we had ordered, or not ordered, at the street stall.

In came a grim looking officer. Dressed in a well-cut civilian suit and wearing very dark designer sun glasses, he barked staccato orders to the policemen around him. They jumped to do whatever he requested. This was a man with considerable power who inspired fear in his subordinates. He sat on a rickety chair facing us and with a stony expression peremptorily questioned Molly. He asked us to identify exactly which dishes we had ordered at the stall and which ones we claimed were delivered. During this process we didn't feel threatened – but neither was it very reassuring.

After ten minutes or so, the food stall owner was frogmarched in by two policemen, who pushed him down onto his knees on the floor in front of us. His head hung low and his eyes fixed to the floor, the man was clearly terrified. Turning his attention to the owner, the officer questioned him in harsh, rasping tones, apparently asking him similar questions about the food ordering. His shoulders slumped miserably. He stuttered his answers while being interrupted impatiently by his interrogator. Even though he had been so hostile towards us, I felt sorry for him. After five minutes, he was dragged out and we were dismissed with the wave of a hand and escorted back to the hotel.

We assumed that was the end of the drama. But at two o'clock in the morning, I was awoken by further knocking on the hotel door. Anxiously I opened up, only to find the manager, two policemen and the forlorn stall owner before me. The manager explained that the case had been decided and that the owner had been found guilty of trying to cheat us. He was therefore obliged to pay us compensation – that was the real value of the meal, about 20 renminbi.

The stall owner looked so wretched that I declined the money, saying that we appreciated that justice had been done and that the compensation wasn't necessary. I thanked the policemen and the manager and the two officers led the stall owner away.

I asked the hotel manager what would happen to him. He said the food stall would certainly lose its licence and would be closed down. The family would not be allowed to open up another and would therefore lose their livelihood. As for the stall owner he may well face a prison sentence.

As we made ready to head back to Hong Kong the next day, our small troop contemplated the previous evening's saga. We wondered why the stall proprietor had tried to cheat us so blatantly. He could easily have overcharged us by local standards, without us realising it. He was taking a huge risk tangling with foreigners in this way, but we assumed it escalated to the point when he was losing face in front of the crowd of spectators and couldn't back down. We also considered the swift but rough justice meted out. Certainly the police were feared, particularly the senior officer, but at least they had protected us, saving us from a dangerous situation and accepting our story.

It was a kind of microcosm of the new China opening up and finding its way in a new open, embryonic capitalist world. This small business saw an opportunity of making quick money, yet the authorities were clearly acting on the basis of making China agreeable to foreign visitors. Tourists were seen as an important long term source of income and such episodes as this did China's image harm. Hence the harsh retribution.

Then there was the educated hotel manager, with his immaculate English and determination to help us. He represented the future China, confident in dealing with the new world and leading the transition of a society from introspection and suspicion to openness and self-confidence.

Our journey back from Shantou to Hong Kong, by bus, was supposed to take seven hours. It took eleven. The bus had hard wooden seats and was driven at reckless speed with continuous use of the horn. Half way to Hong Kong it broke down and the driver explained that we would have to wait for the next one to come along.

This took an hour and when it did arrive we were told we had to pay the full fare again. Protestations proved fruitless, and so we mounted the overcrowded jalopy for the remainder of the bumpy ride to the border. Miraculously, my pregnant wife did not give birth despite the best efforts of the bus driver to induce it.

Finally, exhausted and dehydrated, we reached the border with Hong Kong. As we walked over the check point I reflected how exotic, how alien and challenging Hong Kong had seemed when I had arrived years before. Now, coming out of China proper, Hong Kong was a haven of comfort and familiarity – and we all felt the relief of anyone returning home.

From that time on, whenever I heard the rapid tapping of the Chinese chopper, as neighbours or cooks in restaurants prepared their ingredients, I thought of our misadventure with a little shiver, and welcomed the domesticity the sound now symbolised.

A Brush with Colonial Law

It was just another ordinary evening in Hong Kong. I was driving my family home from a restful afternoon at the expatriate run Hong Kong Football Club, where we had swum, relaxed in the sunshine and eaten – as we often did at the weekend. Such were the pleasures and privileges of expatriate life in the fading years of Hong Kong's colonial era.

The drive home, however, was far from relaxing. As we lived in Tsimshatsui – which is the tip of the mainland peninsula part of Hong Kong – we had to drive from the Island through the Cross Harbour Tunnel to get home. The total distance was only about four miles, but the congestion was at its worst, and it took almost an hour to edge our way beneath the waters of the famous fragrant harbour. It was hot, humid and uncomfortable. The air-conditioner in our old car didn't help much. My wife, with three-month-old daughter, sat in the back, while I tried to negotiate the last mile home through the dense traffic of vehicles and pedestrians. Our baby was uncomfortable and crying.

I was beginning to get very impatient, and my mood deteriorated further with the thought that I had an invite that evening to a stag night of a good friend. At this rate I was going to be late.

To avoid the last half mile of bumper-to-bumper irritation, I decided to take a shortcut via the China Motor Bus depot, a route we frequently used. So began my brief and bizarre acquaintance with the Hong Kong forces of law and order.

As I turned to the exit, to rejoin the main road, I almost ran into a police car parked there, deliberately blocking the slip road. A police constable waved me down to pull in and stop. I wound down the window, not at all perturbed, thinking I would easily pass through by playing the card of ignorance. I was fully aware that our "normal shortcut" through the bus depot was, in fact, illegal – a large sign at the entrance making it clear that only buses were authorised to use this route. However, we, and others, often used this hundred yard stretch of concrete to avoid a particularly busy junction.

"Good evening, Sir," said the smart young Chinese policeman, in his short sleeve green summer uniform. "You are not allowed to come through here. Can I see your driving licence?"

Now this caused a slight complication, because I didn't have a Hong Kong driving licence. I had only bought this car a couple of months previously and just hadn't got round to obtaining one. I had a UK driving licence, though, and had always thought I would be able to bluff my way through any situation like this. There was an element of expatriate smugness in this. Generally, young Chinese policemen found it awkward dealing with English speakers, especially when their own English was limited, and would simply let possible transgressors of traffic law go on their way with a warning.

Unfortunately, this particular constable was fluent and had no such inhibitions. "May I see your Hong Kong licence, Sir?" "Well," I blustered. "I'm just in the process of applying and assume my UK licence covers me in the meantime." None of this was true.

Then the situation took a turn for the worse.

"Please get out of your car, Sir, I am arresting you for driving without a valid licence."

I stepped out, regretting the fact I was now in for a ticket or an on-the-spot fine. But, as it turned out, there was no fine or ticket. I was actually being arrested. This was totally unexpected.

Yes, I would be required to go with the police to the station. No, I would not be allowed to drive my family home. No, my wife could not drive the car home with the baby, because, the constable explained, the car was also "under arrest" as he put it. But surely, I protested, this was a minor traffic offence and there had to be a mistake?

There was no mistake. The police searched me thoroughly, and invited me to climb into the paddy wagon standing open a few yards away. Up to that point there had been an element of farce in the affair, but it took on a more serious turn as I stepped up into the dark interior of the van and they slammed the doors shut.

This action was performed in front of the swelling crowd of thirty to forty jovial Chinese bystanders, who obviously found it hugely entertaining that this Westerner had been caught out for some heinous crime. There was much ribald comment and finger pointing.

Meanwhile, the police gallantly offered my wife, with baby, a lift home – a distance of about two hundred yards. I had assured her that the confusion would soon be sorted out and that I expected to be back home shortly. She was understandably more concerned about the baby's comfort than about my fate.

I was then driven to Kowloon Police Station, which lay only a few miles away. This was one of Hong Kong's main stations. It had a military appearance, with high concrete walls, dotted with crenulated watchtowers at intervals, like a medieval fortress, enclosing a large complex of stern white-plastered buildings, yards and vehicle parks. The semi-military nature of the Hong Kong police force was a result of the serious riots of the late sixties, when Maoist extremists had violently confronted the police and caused serious civil unrest. The British authorities had used troops to contain the trouble.

At this stage I was still unconcerned and more worried about being late for the stag night I'd been invited to that night. It was disquieting, however, when I was shown to a shabby bare room, with an ancient wooden table and three rickety chairs, which was then locked as the unsmiling officer left. I guessed this was an interview room rather than a cell, but it seemed bizarre that I should be locked in. It was slightly Kafkaesque. This was turning into a nightmare. I began to feel distinctly uneasy – how long was I going to be left here under lock and key?

Half an hour later – though it seemed much longer – the door opened. In came a surly looking Chinese sergeant and a cheerful looking younger constable, who offered me tea. Brusquely, the sergeant sat opposite me, opened a log book of some kind, and starting taking my details... name, address and so on.

I asked him if I was really under arrest for a motoring offence? Affirmative. Did arrest mean really under arrest, in that I couldn't go home and would be imprisoned? Affirmative – he nodded without speaking.

"You mean, I can't go home tonight?" I repeated plaintively.

"No go home, you stay here," he added in a bad temper. By then I assumed that his disagreeable mood was partly because he had to deal with a Westerner, and he was not confident with his English language. I guess it was also because it was slightly embarrassing to have to detain me for a trivial offence and answer my questions.

I continued to ask questions, now rather nervously. What was going to happen? What was the charge exactly? Could I call my wife, or a lawyer? Now thoroughly irritated he slammed the book shut, jumped up and stormed out, barking something in Cantonese to the ever-smiling constable.

"He's tired," the constable explained. "He fetches a Scottish officer." Well, that was interesting. The sergeant, fed up of dealing with this troublesome European, was fetching an English speaker, and this particular English speaker was Scottish. I felt comforted, because I assumed the Scot would understand my predicament and surely confirm that there had been some mistranslation, or at least misunderstanding, to explain my bureaucratic predicament.

However, it was not so simple. John McGregor, who looked about twenty years old, with boyish freckled features and the conventional red hair of a Celt, made it clear to me, with considerable politeness, that I was indeed under full arrest. He apologised for this anachronism in Hong Kong law, which, as he admitted, lagged thirty years behind traffic law in the UK, and Scotland. It looked as though I was to be detained at his Excellency's (the Hong Kong Governor and the Queen's representative) pleasure. However, his demeanour gave me hope that some way out existed, as he delivered this information in a friendly, confidential way.

Sure enough, when I enquired if I needed a lawyer again, he offered the escape route.

"That's probably not necessary. You will be charged, and obliged to appear before magistrate's court in due course, but in the meantime you can just pay the statutory bail and then go home," he comforted me.

It turned out that I could purchase my freedom, however temporary, for two thousand Hong Kong dollars – a considerable sum in those days, equal roughly to two hundred pounds. There was only one slight hitch. I didn't have two thousand dollars on me. This presented an interesting Catch 22 situation, for when I requested permission to leave the station to get the cash from an automated cash machine, a device already quite ubiquitous in technology obsessed Hong Kong, my erstwhile Scottish saviour replied: "No, I'm afraid you can't leave the station – you are under arrest."

"So I can't leave to get the cash that would enable me to leave?" I repeated. "Not even with an escort?" "Afraid not," he confirmed, "And anyway, you will have to give a statement first, then perhaps you can call your wife to come with the bail money." And with that, he left.

At least having been offered an escape route, I calmly sat and awaited my next instructions. After a few moments, that same cheerful young Chinese constable came in with the same angelic smile, carrying an antiquated and battered manual typewriter, circa 1950s. As this was already the dawn of computers, for word processing at least, the appearance of this ancient apparatus did not bode well for efficient statement taking.

The constable settled himself opposite me, and, taking pains to insert a pristine sheet of white paper, began to type something with two index fingers. Presumably a heading.

He then began. "So Mr Wingate, please tell me what happened, leading to your arrest." I took a deep breath and chose my words carefully.

"I was returning home from Hong Kong to Tsimshatsui, when I noticed the traffic at the junction at the end of University Road was particularly congested, so I decided to take a short cut through..." At this point he interrupted me.

"One moment please... I...was...returning....what was next?" His understanding of my English was first class, but his two finger typing was obviously going to make this a very tedious exercise. My heart sank. The time was now eight-o-clock. I had been at the station about two hours. My stag night was now under serious threat.

I think I gave one of the most direct, succinct and suppliant confessions ever given in a Hong Kong police station. It was short, largely monosyllabic, with mainly three word sentences. It took one and a half hours. Throughout, the constable smiled patiently and typed intently but incompetently.

When he finally pulled out the completed document with a triumphant flourish, he had no idea of the torture he had inflicted on me. He showed me my "confession". It was littered with mistyping, misspelling and crossings out with an x. Kowloon police station was obviously pre-Tippex, never mind word processing. Despite the fact the shoddy document was evidence of both my guilt and my illiteracy, I signed it willingly.

I then called my wife. She had to arrange a baby-sitter, go out to find a cash machine, then hail a taxi, and finally make her way to the station, which was only a half-hour drive from our flat. Of course this took time, and I am suspicious to this day that she did not rush on account of schadenfreude she felt for me missing my stag night, of which she had never entirely approved, given the dubious reputation of the crowd attending.

After a further two hours, at about 11:30 pm, I was finally released from custody, when my wife handed over the blood money. We were pleasantly surprised to hear from the sergeant, who was by then in a better mood, that we could take the offending car, as long as my wife drove. He pointed out that I would in due course be sent an invitation to attend Court to receive my punishment, and that I would be in serious trouble if I attempted to drive again without a proper Hong Kong licence.

We sheepishly took our departure, shaking hands with the young constable, who grinned in approval at our release. As my wife drove cautiously out of the station, we were amused to notice that as we passed through the huge wrought iron gates that guarded the entrance, the two armed policemen standing on sentry boxes either side stood to attention and saluted us with great formality.

It almost equalled the irony of the fact that my wife wasn't in possession of a valid Hong Kong licence either. She is a German national and had neither Hong Kong nor British licence. But at least I was a free man!

About three months later I received a summons to appear at Kowloon Magistrates Court. I had no idea of what to expect in terms of the procedures, but I had, in the meantime, been assured by friends serving in the Hong Kong police force, that my punishment would most likely be a fine – possibly as much as two thousand Hong Kong dollars. This was a significant sum, but better than being detained again! I had also made sure that my wife and I were now in possession of a legitimate Hong Kong driving licence.

Kowloon Magistrates Court lay in the heart of Kowloon – the main urban area on the Hong Kong peninsula. It was a rather foreboding, large brick building going back to the early 20th century.

I arrived well in time on the appointed day and checked in at the desk. The reception area was scruffy and it was very busy, with the Chinese desk sergeant and constables obviously under pressure to process the queues. I quickly noticed that I was the only European present, and was attracting some curious looks. The sergeant took my details officiously and pointed to a large double door.

I had expected a small room, with few people and a rapid, informal process, at which I would plead guilty, be quickly admonished by a magistrate, arbitrarily fined and summarily dismissed. Probably, all over in ten minutes.

However, when I stepped into the courtroom, this was clearly not going to be the case. I found myself in a huge auditorium, with tiered rows of wooden bench seats, like a lecture hall. It was built to seat several hundred people and, indeed, about two hundred were there already, chatting loudly. On the floor of the hall was a raised dais, some four feet high, with a large desk in the centre, and other desks on either side. Clearly, this was for the magistrate and his assistants. Everyone there was Chinese – and most of them were elderly, with the majority being women dressed in traditional black tunics and trousers.

When I entered there was a distinct hush and everyone looked around. There was certain amount of pointing and whispering. I felt very self-conscious and slipped onto the nearest vacant bench near the back, as if I were an errant student who had crept conspicuously late into a lecture.

Ten minutes later, the clerks of the court trooped in and took their positions. They wore court gowns, but not wigs. One stood up and requested us rise in Cantonese and English. Everyone took to their feet and in swept our Magistrate. I was struck immediately by the fact that he was a Caucasian and that he was young. I guessed late thirties. I assumed from his accent later he was from New Zealand. It gave me a sense of ethnic comfort that my crime would be better tolerated. He allowed us to sit down again, and so the institution of Colonial Law swung into action.

One of the court clerks, who was clearly also the interpreter, announced in a pompous official voice the first case in Cantonese, and then in English for the magistrate's and my benefit.

"Miss Wong Kar-chan is accused of illegally hawking in Mongkok, without a licence, on March 13. Miss Wong has 74 previous convictions. She pleads guilty."

The recidivist felon, Miss Wong, stood up from the benches. She was about five feet tall and somewhere in the region of seventy years old. She wore the traditional garb of black tunic and short baggy trousers. On her feet wooden-soled

134

sandals. She clattered her way unsteadily down from the benches to the floor of the auditorium on thin, bandy legs.

Once down, however, all signs of timidity vanished. First, she bowed deeply three times before the magistrate as if she was in a Chinese temple before her gods. Then, she hurled herself prone to the floor in front of the magistrate's dais, and launched into a wailing speech at high volume. While screeching at the top of her voice, she beat the wooden floor with her fists and, intermittently, her forehead.

No-one moved to help her or intervene. The bench and clerks sat impassively, making notes. The crowd murmured in sympathy or approval at Miss Wong's tragic monologue. Of course, I didn't understand a word, but help was at hand.

Once the defendant had finished, she stood up again, and waited with bowed head and hands behind her back like a recalcitrant schoolchild. The interpreter explained.

"Miss Wong is very sorry for her misdemeanour. She begs to explain to the magistrate that she only hawks in extreme cases. She is very poor and so is her family. She supports a family of 23 people and this is the only way she can make any income as she is too old to get a proper job. She hopes that the court can forgive her and understand her hard life."

Silence. The magistrate was making a few notes. Finally, he gave his verdict. It was perfunctory and without context.

"Fifty dollars fine," he said, not looking up and with the air of a man terminally bored. A man who had heard it all before.

Miss Wong greeted this judgement as a great victory for natural justice. She smiled broadly, exhibiting at least three gold teeth and bowed repeatedly before the magistrate. Her entourage began to applaud, before being summarily silenced by the magistrate with a sharp rap of his gavel.

"Next case!" he intoned. Miss Wong was gently led away from her robotic bowing, surrounded by supporters and borne away to general approval.

The clerk began the next case.

"Miss Cheung Mei-yee is accused of illegally hawking in Tsimshatsui, without a licence, on April 24. Miss Cheung has 86 previous convictions. She pleads guilty."

Miss Cheung, who was obviously even further beyond rehabilitation than Miss Wong, was of similar outlook and demeanour. She had apparently learnt her courtroom behaviour from a similar manual. She also kowtowed before the magistrate, and similarly softened our hearts with her tale of hardship and large, impoverished family. The performance ended in tears.

"Fifty dollars fine," droned the magistrate after thirty seconds consideration. Clearly these cases must have made him reflect on the value of the years of obtuse legal training he had endured to be able to make a real difference to society. Miss Cheung was triumphant, however.

And so the morning proceeded. I had arrived at about 9:30 in the morning. By about 11:00 we had probably heard a dozen hawking cases. All criminals were elderly men or women. All pleaded guilty. All had tales of misery and misfortune. All were fined 50 dollars.

At first I had found this fascinating and mildly amusing. However, after Mr Chan Chi-choi had been fined 50 dollars for hawking in Yaumatei, I was finding it as repetitive as the magistrate, and wondering when I would be called. My penitent performance would no doubt be a huge disappointment to the still large crowd. It was, indeed, a kind of theatre, and I would be judged a complete bore.

Then came a dramatic interlude. Instead of a hawking case the clerk announced that Mr Yeung Wai-man and Mr Fong

Chi-doi were accused of kidnapping. This was serious crime. The two defendants, definitely not seated among the "audience", were led into the dock, positioned at the edge of the floor, from a side door. Accompanied by four uniformed officers, they were handcuffed. They looked young, grubby and forlorn – and not at all in my image of dangerous triads or Chinese gangsters.

An officer was summoned to provide evidence, all of which was patiently translated by the court officer, sentence by sentence. At last the magistrate sat up and paid close attention, clearly re-animated by the prospect of a more demanding intellectual challenge.

It was a pathetic story. It transpired that these two delinquents, who were in their late teens, had kidnapped a businessman in their locality. Like any kidnapping, it had a vicious aspect. They had taken him prisoner by threatening him with Chinese choppers, bound him and incarcerated him in a flat nearby. They had telephoned his family and demanded money. The amateurish nature of their criminality became obvious, for they only demanded five thousand Hong Kong dollars, which being equivalent to about five hundred pounds, was hardly worth risking going to prison for.

Even more ridiculously, they had told the family where to meet them face-to-face with the ransom money. Consequently, the family informed the police, who easily detained them at the agreed rendezvous point. Fortunately, the kidnap victim was unhurt and had only suffered detention for a couple of hours, though of course it would have been a harrowing experience for him and his family.

The magistrate pointed out the serious nature of the crime and commented on the youth and ineptitude of the defendants. He ordered them sent on to the Crown Court for trial by jury. I don't suppose that trial was complex or lengthy.

After the tension of a real criminal case the assembled ·gallery were then treated to a further spectacle – a westerner in trouble! What could he have done?

The clerk introduced my case.

"Mr Frank Wingate, accused of driving without a valid Hong Kong driving licence in Tsimshatsui, on March 12. Mr Wingate pleads guilty." The magistrate looked up, curious that a westerner was appearing before him. I walked down to the front, consciously keeping my dignity intact. I did not bow, nor spreadeagle myself on the floor. I did, however, acknowledge the magistrate with a dignified inclination of the head.

The clerk continued with a few details of the case. How I had been stopped and arrested, and how I had made my statement and paid bail. He then asked me again how I pleaded.

"Guilty, your honour," I replied with firmness and a hint of supplication.

The magistrate paused a moment, looked at me and smiled.

"Mr Wingate, you don't have to call me your honour. You can address me as "Sir". I am not a judge. Mr Wingate, don't you have anything to say for yourself?"

This took me by surprise as I assumed mine was a cut and dried affair, but I accepted this offer to explain the mitigating circumstances behind my misdemeanour. At each point the clerk interpreted it for the attentive and curious assembly. The theme of my impromptu defence was as follows:

"You see, Sir, I had assumed that my English driving licence was still valid in Hong Kong. I had only bought my car six months before and I thought that my English driving licence would cover me for at least six months."

Warming to my case and imitating the themes of my fellow defendants that morning I played the family card too.

"Also, Sir, I was driving my wife and small child – only three months old. She was clearly unwell and my wife was distraught. I thought in the circumstances, and to save time, it would be OK to cut through the bus station."

The magistrate was understanding in a sort of patronising way.

"Mr Wingate you are indeed correct that an English driving licence is valid in Hong Kong for a period of six months immediately following the arrival of the owner of that licence in Hong Kong."

"How long have you been in Hong Kong, Mr Wingate?"

"Fourteen years, sir," I replied shamefacedly.

"Quite," he said.

"Mr Wingate, given your clean record hitherto and your admission of guilt, I will be lenient this time. You are fined eight hundred Hong Kong dollars."

He tapped his gavel and that was that. I was shown out, given a form of invoice, told to pay within seven days, and released into the sunshine. My fine was substantial but bearable and much less than the potential maximum of two thousand.

I had briefly experienced British colonial law with all its foibles. Theatrical, pompous, diffident, but impartial and ultimately tolerant and humane. My greatest regret was missing the stag night. To my disappointment, I had learnt that it had been an exceptionally decadent and enjoyable evening.

Great Expectorations

After the din of traffic and heavy pollution of Tsimshatsui, Hong Kong's mainland peninsula, our new flat in Wang Fung Terrace, Tai Hang Road, on the island itself, was a haven of peace and fresh air. Not more than five minutes walk from the bizarre tourist attraction of Tiger Balm Gardens, Wang Fung Terrace nestled high on the hillside, above the valley of Sukunpoo.

My wife and I and two children had moved back to the island after more than a year living in a flat on the mainland, next to the entrance of the cross-harbour road tunnel. There we had enjoyed subsidised accommodation – a modern and spacious flat – provided by the Hong Kong Polytechnic, my wife's employer.

Unfortunately the luxury of the interior was not matched by the environment, for tens of thousands of cars queued day and night to enter the tunnel, just a few hundred feet away. The continuous drone and exhaust emissions were only excluded from the flat by having the windows permanently closed and the air conditioner running.

So, mindful of the health of our new born daughter, we took a more expensive option and rented the Wang Fung Terrace flat. It was a three bedroom place, comfortable, light and airy, and, above all, peaceful. The five storey block was over thirty years old and perched precariously on the terrace, which had been carved out of the mountainside. From the balcony at the front, we could see far and wide, through trees, to the Government Sports Stadium in the valley below. On a clear day, we could catch a glimpse of Hong Kong Harbour.

Our mainly Chinese neighbours were amicable and reserved and we soon settled down into a pleasant routine. This happy state continued for some two years, when an unexpected intrusion into our contented mode of life disturbed the peace and caused disturbance and dismay. It was the appearance of the serial spitter.

I'm not precious about the act of clearing one's throat and spitting. I had got used to the fact that in Hong Kong, the older generation of Chinese still spat in public more than was common back home. I can well remember in public toilets in the UK in the fifties signs reading "Do not spit. Spitting causes TB". For a young boy they were quite alarming and I assumed that if I spat, then I might spread TB. But social pressure was such that the habit, in public at least, was frowned upon and rarely seen.

But social change in Hong Kong was still in progress and there were frequent public signs discouraging the habit. The younger generation in general did not spit, though I did notice early on a greater toleration. I was surprised in my first teaching job at a Chinese school, that the boys would request to go to the toilet in order to "clear their throat".

However, the problem at Wang Fung Terrace began with the arrival of the new watchman. Ah Fung, as we later learned his name to be, or Mr Fung, was appointed to guard our block, number five. This in itself was an unnecessary and ineffective human resource deployment.

For a start, Wang Fung Terrace was a narrow road, which was quite hard to access and certainly off the beaten track. Furthermore, number five, our block, was right at the top of the terrace, and anyone with evil intent would have to pass along the two hundred metres of the Terrace undetected. Even then the block had a lobby which was permanently locked. Each of us residents had our own key.

Certainly, for us, the employment of a watchman made no sense. However, the residents' association had decided that it was needed and would guarantee our security. At this time the association was heavily influenced by the articulate and urbane Dr Chan, who lived in the flat below us.

I suspect that the decision to install Ah Fung was more to do with status and perception than security. Number 5 Wang Fung Terrace had indeed undergone significant upgrading in the two years we lived there. This was due to the influx of younger, wealthier professional Chinese couples, who were benefiting from the property boom then engulfing Hong Kong. Flats, even in relative backwaters like Wang Fung Terrace, could easily double in value in two or three years, and people were buying, investing in upgrades and then moving on with profitable rapidity. Poor old Ah Fung was an unwitting player in this property carousel. His presence was designed to add even more value to Dr Chan's flat and those of other owners.

He didn't really fit the bill. Many smarter blocks around town had watchmen and security staff, often uniformed and swaggering, with all the self-endowed importance of a petty official. But Ah Fung had neither a uniform nor swagger. From the beginning he sat forlornly in a telephone box size hut at the entrance to our block. He had no traffic barrier to operate, nor equipment – except for an old-style black telephone.

He sat on a rickety bar stool in his shelter, dressed usually in a grubby string vest, staring into space and listening to a battered old transistor radio, that played non-stop discordant Cantonese pop music or opera. It seemed as though he remained there almost permanently, only occasionally disappearing to relieve himself and get something to eat.

Ah Fung was elderly – well into his seventies I would guess, and incredibly weatherbeaten. He had probably been a farmer in his day, and was then, like many old folk in Hong Kong, barely eking out a living in that unforgiving capitalist city. He was not unfriendly, but didn't speak a single word of English and certainly didn't understand any. This was not a problem, for we were one of only two non-Chinese residents in the block. He would nod politely when we passed, but I rarely saw him smile. He looked upon us with curiosity and apprehension.

Soon after he appeared an unfortunate incident occurred which would have strengthened his suspicion of foreigners and particularly of me. This happened after an alcoholic evening at the Foreign Correspondents Club, my wife's and my favourite bar. On that evening, we had been celebrating my gaining membership.

After a celebratory evening, we didn't get home and to bed until the early hours. Some time later, in the middle of the night, I got up, feeling, unsurprisingly, dehydrated and in need of a glass of water. I fumbled my way to the kitchen, in the pitch black, not wanting to wake up my wife or children. I went through the door to the kitchen and obtained the necessary liquid. I then returned through the kitchen door in a half-comatose state.

I was surprised when the door sprang shut behind me, and even more surprised that the living room light was on. Then I quite suddenly sobered up to the realisation that I was outside the flat in the main stairwell. Our kitchen had two doors – one connecting to the living room and one to the outside world. In my sleepy stupor I had emerged into the public realm. This in itself would not have posed a major problem had I possessed a shred of clothing. However, I was as naked as Adam, without even a fig leaf to cover my modesty.

I immediately turned round to our front door and tapped gently on it, hoping to rouse my wife. No success. I tapped louder and then knocked. No success – she was in a deep and contented sleep. Then my panic grew as I heard a couple coming up the stairs. We were on the third floor of a five storey block and there was no lift. They were going to pass within a few feet of me.

Turning my face to the wall I tried to merge into the shadows. I covered my privacy with both hands. As the couple passed I closed my eyes. They paused momentarily, having obviously seen me, stopped talking for a moment, and then, with welcome Chinese reserve and sang-froid, just carried on. No reaction.

The momentary relief from embarrassment was swiftly replaced by further panic. What on earth was I going to do?

Trying to be logical, I thought I must get to a phone to wake my wife. Before I could get to a phone I needed something to cover my nakedness. Where could I find any kind of clothing? Then I remembered that some of our neighbours hung their washing out to dry on the roof of the building. Problem was that the door to the roof was often locked and that there was no guarantee that I would find any suitable attire hanging there.

Nevertheless, it was my only chance and I slunk guiltily up the stairwell to the roof. Luckily, it was open, and there was clothing. Feeling like a pervert I hastily snatched a voluminous pair of polkadot underpants, at least four sizes too big for me, and a large red and white striped bath towel. Nervous that I might be caught and accused of being a kinky underwear thief I slipped back inside.

My first concern was to get to the nearest phone box. The only one I could think of was at least half a mile away on the main road. But then I had a brainwave. There was surely a phone in the watchman's booth! By this time dawn was just beginning to rise and the first light crept through the windows.

Cautiously, I crept down the stairs and into the building forecourt. In the dim light I could see Ah Fung, clearly arriving to begin his shift. Throwing reserve to the wind I marched up to the watchman's booth and in my boldest Cantonese asked to use the ancient telephone.

From Ah Fung's astonished and fearful reaction, I could tell that my sudden appearance shook him to the core. He no doubt thought I was a white apparition or ghost coming from the shadows; possibly an Indian mahatma; definitely a madman. This visitation no doubt negatively influenced his subsequent and long lasting impression of my character and status – an indelible impression that probably reinforced his prejudice about crazy foreigners.

His jaw dropped and his eyes opened wide. He nodded, stepped aside, moved to a safe distance and pointed to the phone. As I called home he watched in amazement. Within a few minutes I had successfully aroused my wife, who was highly amused and totally unsympathetic. My situation was rescued, but the psychological damage done to Ah Fung was irreparable.

Some weeks after he had taken up his post to guard us against crime and lawlessness, Ah Fung started to indulge in an unfortunate habit that was to cause dissension within the block – namely an excessively loud, extended and repetitive throat clearing exercise. This was done with such vigour, lack of self-consciousness and social sensitivity as to be a mystery to this day.

Some people whistle to pass the time. Others hum. Ah Fung hawked. He hawked and spat in the evenings at least once an hour, with each session lasting some ten minutes and culminating in an audible expectoration of significant proportions and volume.

I'm not the squeamish sort, and it wasn't the process itself, but the intensity and frequency of the exercise that had a disturbing effect. On the balmy Hong Kong evenings of that Autumn, we, along with other neighbours, would leave windows and balcony doors wide open to catch a little fresh air, rather than relying totally on air conditioning. As Ah Fung was only 30 feet directly below us, his evening performance was very intrusive.

For the first few evenings, we inclined to ignore it, reasoning the poor old fellow probably had a bad cold or a sore throat and that the habit was temporary. When it became obvious this was not the case, I would go to the balcony, lean over and shout down politely, in a very English way: "Excuse me! Could you stop that please!", or some such phrase. This might have had a very short term effect, but the motor soon revved up again.

After a week or so it was becoming less of a joke. The tearing, buzz-saw sound of Ah Fung clearing his sinuses was interrupting favourite television programmes or family dinner conversations. For the children, the theatre was quite amusing. Our nine year old boy would rush to the balcony to imitate and partner Ah Fung in his dissonant activity. Our three year old 'girl would run around the flat, clapping gleefully, when Ah Fung started up, shouting happily, "Mama, he's doing it! He's doing it again," knowing this would wind up her mother considerably.

My wife, who is German, and possessing that German attribute of forthright expression, also took to leaning over the balcony to remonstrate with the incomprehending janitor. Good taste would prevent me from directly translating the colourful Rhineland phraseology, which was of course entirely wasted on its Cantonese victim.

Our American neighbour, Lindy, who lived in the flat below us, and was therefore even closer to the offending evening symphony, took to direct action also. We would hear her nasal New York shriek piercing the calm evening of our terrace community. "Shut the fuck up!" was her favourite admonition.

Lindy Feinstein was quite a strange person. We befriended her early on, but kept the relationship at a healthy arm's length, because she was neurotic. She would bang on our door unannounced, flounce in and throw herself to the floor in our living room, whatever we were doing, and, sitting cross-legged, and smoking compulsively, would tell us of the latest emotional disaster to befall her – at great length. We would be subject to intense monologues, of usually quite intimate nature and at least an hour in length.

These intense outpourings would consist of extensive complaints about the nature of her existence. Her life was truly awful. She didn't like Asia, especially Hong Kong. Her job – she was an interior designer to very wealthy people, who were obviously impossible and feckless clients – was a torture. And her relationship with Chuck, her partner, was, needless to say, a tragedy. Their sex life? A story of misunderstanding and failed expectation.

This was all revealed to us, despite the fact that Chuck appeared to be quiet, polite, hard-working and, clearly, devoted to his unhinged girlfriend. Chuck was a financier of some kind – dull and intelligent. After listening to Lindy, you would imagine him to be a fiend and psychological abuser. Lindy's monologues would end abruptly, my wife having listened politely and delivered her at least two large glasses of wine, with a sudden "Great to talk to you guys!". Then she would leap up and sashay out.

Even Lindy's coarse tirades did little to deter Ah Fung. The lengthy hawking and spitting interludes continued – ever more irritating. I did confront Ah Fung, and tried to explain in broken Cantonese, with accompanying gestures and sound effects, that he should refrain from this habit. But it was to no avail. Ah Fung didn't understand one word, and, anyway, he obviously considered me mentally unbalanced.

After two weeks of this, we reluctantly went to the block's residents' association. We had never attended this, partly because we were tenants rather than owners, and partly because we assumed it was a Cantonese language affair, all other residents there being Chinese apart from ourselves and Lindy.

I approached our neighbour below, Dr Chan – a dapper medical doctor, who was chair of the association. Whilst being sympathetic and attentive, he surprisingly denied all knowledge of the problem. Meanwhile, he invited me to express my concerns at the association meeting the very next evening.

Although slightly nervous and feeling like an interloper with a petty problem, I did attend and found the other residents to be kind and receptive. However, they too did not recognise Ah Fung's behaviour as a problem. So the old man did spit occasionally? Well, he was a simple soul and meant no harm. Nor did they agree with me that a watchman was unnecessary. It was obvious to them that security was essential and that Ah Fung was better than nothing, and, indeed, an inexpensive solution. It was agreed that Dr Chan would have a quiet word with Ah Fung. By the end of my attendance at the meeting I felt as though I was victimising the old watchman.

Whatever Mr Chan said to Ah Fung, if anything at all, had only a short-term effect and soon he was once again terrorising us with his rasping crescendos.

Then finally I thought I had found the solution. I asked my Chinese colleagues at work – a PR company – for their advice. They suggested a polite letter that I might hand direct to Ah Fung. They listened to the whole tale and composed in neat Chinese characters a request to Ah Fung to cease his habitual hawking. This letter I handed myself to Ah Fung that very evening. He received it quizzically, only glancing at it momentarily before stuffing it unceremoniously in his back trouser pocket. That should do the trick I thought, without offending him in any way.

Unfortunately, my strategy seemed to have no effect, for the hawking continued – at least for another week. And then, quite suddenly, Ah Fung was gone. His plastic watchman's box was empty and quiet.

When I next met Mr Chan, I asked what had happened, concerned that my letter had caused Ah Fung to leave. "Oh, don't worry about that," he replied, "The old man was completely illiterate – he couldn't have read one character of any letter."

"No," continued, Mr Chan, in a diffident tone, "He just failed to turn up again. I heard he was ill and has gone back to China to die."

Our next watchman, Ah Yeung, did not spit noisily. He did, however, listen to his transistor radio at top volume, particularly to high pitched, hysterical horse-racing commentary. We heard no more of Ah Fung, but I felt a little guilty when I thought of him.

Philippina Maid

Sharing the family name of one of the Philippines' great heroes, who gave his life opposing the dictator Marcos, Evelyn Aquino was unprepossessing, shy and very nervous when she came for her interview.

Who could blame her? So much depended on getting this job as our live-in maid in Hong Kong. Her daughter, for one, back in the Philippines; and her family, who relied on her remittances. She was just one of tens of thousands who came to Hong Kong to seek relief from the poverty and lack of opportunity in their bountiful but benighted homeland. We could have chosen from a hundred applicants had we wished.

For us, as expatriates in the UK's last serious colony, having a live-in domestic help was quite normal. Everyone in Hong Kong with their own home, however small, and a reasonable income, Chinese and expatriate, had a live-in.

Evelyn suited us well. Her main responsibility was to care for our nine-year-old son and baby daughter, and we assessed that she had the kindness, gentleness and patience that we wanted. After a simple and short interview we hired her.

Amahs are live in maids or nannies, who help take care of the home and sometimes children. There was a long tradition of amahs in Chinese society, the role often being taken by adopted children or single women who for one reason or another chose not to marry. Famously the "black and white" amahs of Chinese tradition wore those colours and were respected members of the family.

In Hong Kong in the 1970s there were few Chinese amahs left, and as the middle class grew and prospered on the back of economic success, more Philippinas were recruited via agencies to fulfil the role. For expats and Chinese residents alike they were affordable and willing. At the time the going rate for a live-in was about three thousand Hong Kong dollars a month (roughly £250). While this was a pittance compared to average Hong Kong salaries, it was equivalent to a decent middle management income in Manila.

These women had a tough life. Most of them worked six days a week for their Hong Kong employers, from morning till night, responsible for housekeeping, childcare and cooking. The vast majority were probably treated respectfully, but there were cases of maltreatment and exploitation that came to light. Stories emerged of women sleeping on the floor in kitchens, and occasionally being beaten or sexually abused.

The problem was they had little legal protection. Treated as non-residents, they were employed on contract, usually on an annual basis. If they lost their job, they would most likely be on the next plane home. However awful their conditions, their income was a lifeline for impoverished families back home, and they couldn't jeopardise that by complaining! Normally, as part of that contract, they would receive a ticket home once every two years, so this often divided them from their families and children for years at a time.

Their numbers grew throughout the boom years of the 1980s until they formed the largest expatriate community. By the time we left Hong Kong in 2000, Philippinas working in Hong Kong numbered over 140,000.

The general reputation of these hard-working women among expatriates was far from negative. Whether inspired by their fatalistic Catholic faith or just natural disposition, Philippinas were usually cheerful, smiling, party loving and optimistic.

For younger single Brits, like myself in the earlier years, they made companiable, easy-going girlfriends. Certain bars, like the Makati Inn, named after a district in Manila, was a popular hangout for Philippinas at the weekend and a magnet for red-blooded males in search of female company. Several of my friends married Philippinas and enjoyed happy lifelong partnerships.

It was an established part of the Hong Kong Sunday scene, to see tens of thousands of Philippinas gathering in public parks and spaces, where they would congregate to eat, gossip and often sing. It was a colourful scene, with the rat-a-tat-tat of Tagalog chatter sounding like a vast flock of birds. The community was always nourished by numerous platefuls of lumpiah (spring rolls), fried chicken, noodles and fried rice.

Evelyn settled in with us quickly, rapidly becoming a part of the family. Unlike many other amahs she was not expected to cook. My wife prepared the family meals in the evening. This was just as well, as we soon discovered that her culinary skills were non-existent.

Suspicions were first aroused about this lack of kitchen craft, when, in the early days, our cheese selection in the fridge disappeared over night. After the second incident, when the Camembert, Roquefort, Stilton and other exotic cheeses went missing again, we asked Evelyn if she was involved.

"Why of course," she replied, perplexed, "It was rotten and smelt bad, so I threw it out before it made everything else stink."

A year on in her role and a greater challenge presented itself when my wife went on a short holiday with our daughter. This left Evelyn to prepare one dinner for myself and our son. Not wanting to make it difficult I suggested a simple fare of roast chicken, baked beans and chips.

It was the strangest outcome. The chicken was presented on a serving dish – complete with head and feet. It was the most emaciated excuse for a chicken I had ever seen. There was simply no meat on it. It was all bone, skin and sinew. We picked at it politely, but the pretence couldn't last and I tossed it in the bin when Evelyn had gone out. Poor woman had been totally ripped off at the local Chinese market, where she was a complete novice.

Bizarrely, she managed to burn the baked beans also, as well as the chips. This was an unknown level of incompetence. The beans were left too long and the bottom 25 percent turned black. As for the chips, Evelyn used raw fresh potato when she should have used the oven ready version. So her efforts also turned black on the outside while staying raw on the inside.

However, this was all inconsequential, for more importantly she proved a kind and patient carer to our son and daughter. Our son liked her very much, despite complaining gently on occasions that his school sandwiches were unappetizing.

For Sophie, our baby, Evelyn, or "Arbie" as she called her, was a major factor in her infancy and growing to awareness. Although we were busy parents, both pursuing careers, we always found time to be home in the evenings. But for the rest of the day, there was Evelyn, cooing, coaxing, singing and talking to our child and keeping her safe.

Once or twice linguistic confusion amused us. At dinner one evening, the eighteen month old Sophie began shouting happily. "Arsehole!" she chirped. "Arsehole!" "Arsehole!"

Suspicion immediately fell on her brother, who was told off for mischievously teaching his little sister crude words. He, however, while finding it extremely funny, denied any involvement. Evelyn, who was nearby, overheard this and explained that "Aso" was Tagalog for dog, and Sophie, who had picked this up from Evelyn, was merely responding to the loud barking of some mongrel outside!

Another time, we asked Sophie what she and Evelyn had had for lunch that day. "Pish Pilay" she answered. "I like Pish Pilay". They ate this dish, which we presumed was some Philippine speciality – like pork adobo – quite often and Sophie had clearly acquired a taste for it.

We asked Evelyn for the recipe, but it proved quite an anti-climax when we first came to understand this was in fact "Fish Fillet" – the soft "F" sound not being a consonant used in Tagalog. Any hopes of an exotic seafood dish were then further punctured when Evelyn appeared with a packet of Birds Eye fish fingers from the kitchen. Yes, Pish Pilay was Fish Fingers.

A couple of years rolled by in Hong Kong, and my career and my wife's prospered. Social life was rich and entertaining. Our children grew up with the support of Evelyn. She stayed as faithful, sweet-natured and reliable as ever. We counted ourselves lucky to benefit from her work. Soon Sophie was going to school and our son was already in secondary education.

Then, quite unexpectedly, we started to receive strange phone calls in the evening, intermittently at first. A voice would ask for Evelyn. This wasn't entirely unusual, except, being in pre-mobile days, Evelyn actually had her own phone line and number in her room and her friends would normally call her direct, not use the family number. Also, it was strange for a man to call, as most of her friends were female maids like her.

We mentioned this to her, but she brushed off the calls at first, although obviously embarrassed. We assumed she had some kind of admirer, but this seemed unlikely. She asked us just to say that she was out. Then, gradually, over a period of weeks, the calls became more frequent, and more aggressive.

We would ask who was calling and they would hang up. Evelyn, meanwhile, continued to protest her ignorance as to the source of this calls, despite the fact they became a nuisance.

Then, at a certain point, the tone changed and became menacing. As we reacted with annoyance, the callers, usually male, began to make accusations about Evelyn. Did we know she was sleeping around? Did we know she was a whore? A drug addict? Had we checked around the house that nothing had been stolen?

We had no doubt these calls were malicious and designed to blacken her character with us. But why? Initial confrontations with Evelyn only produced denials and claims of mistaken identity. No, she knew nothing of this and it was just other Philippinas causing trouble for her. Her fellow countrywomen, she told us, were terrible gossips and it could be a case of jealousy on account of her comfortable job with us.

A month after the calls first began, however, our questions became persistent. The dam of her resistance finally broke and in a tearful confession we learned the story of her problem – or at least most of it.

She was in debt – heavily in debt – and these calls were from the loan agency putting pressure on her to pay up. We were shocked, not so much that anyone could fall into debt, but that Evelyn – innocent, naïve, sensible Evelyn – had got herself into this hole. As the story unfolded, it took on familiar characteristics. Like many of her co-patriots working in Hong Kong, she had been heavily pressured by her family for more and more money. These hard working women were seen as wealthy cash cows by their impoverished families back home and they were put under continuous moral blackmail.

Evelyn's tale was typical. Her father was elderly and ill and had not worked for some years. Her brother was a heroin addict. His wife had a small baby and the baby had been ill. Money was needed for Evelyn's mother to look after Evelyn's daughter by her earlier marriage. Money was needed to look after the father, the addicted brother and his family and sick child. Evelyn's husband was never mentioned and clearly not on the scene.

She explained that most of her salary went back home. Of course, she had few running costs in Hong Kong, being housed and fed by us, and having a very modest social life. Nevertheless, the remittances were obviously not enough. Perhaps the brother was wasting the money on drugs. We did learn from Evelyn later that her baby niece had died from lack of medicine as the brother had frittered away the funds she sent on his drug habit.

As a result, and being dutiful, Evelyn had borrowed money from a loans agency in Hong Kong to supplement her remittances and over a couple of years this had built up. Now there was a crisis. She revealed to us that she had a further serious problem. The loans agency had possession of her passport, which they had taken as surety, so she couldn't even return to the Philippines that summer as scheduled. She was marooned in Hong Kong.

She told us that she was HK$16,000 in debt, more than five times her monthly salary. This put us in a quandary. We wanted to help and decided immediately we would pay off some of the debt for her. Evelyn was part of the family and we wanted to keep her. But we were reluctant to pay it all as we guessed that this situation would simply arise again. My wife and I agreed to pay HK$10,000 of her debt on the condition that we withdrew a small proportion from her monthly salary to pay off the rest.

But when we put this proposition to Evelyn the result was unexpected. For the first time we saw her angry. No, she would never accept that we docked her salary and this was none of our business. Furious, she accused us of exploiting her and that rather than accepting such a humiliating arrangement she would rather leave right now and return to Manila. This was between her and her family. I had to remind her she couldn't leave Hong Kong without a passport. The result was a collapse amid floods of tears.

After we had comforted her, we assured her we would do everything to help and that we would not force her to do anything against her will. The first step, apart from reducing her debt to more manageable proportions, was to retrieve her passport. Having spoken to a senior police officer friend about the situation the prognosis was complicated.

Yes, he confirmed, it was illegal for anyone to hold someone else's passport against their wishes. However, this was apparently a common story in Hong Kong. Many Philippinas fell into this trap of giving up their passport as surety to loan sharks. Many went to the police for help, but then failed to pursue their case for fear of retribution from the loan sharks. He recommended that I, as an expat, would have more sway with the police if I accompanied Evelyn.

Two days later a defeated Evelyn and I went to the main police station in Mid-Levels Hong Kong. She was reluctant to go, even in her hopeless predicament. In the dismal, whitewashed surroundings of the station, I explained the case to the Chinese sergeant and constable on duty. They were unfriendly, and clearly regarded the matter as familiar and predictable.

Speaking to Evelyn in an unkind tone, they asked if she was in debt, and why she had handed over her passport, implying this was entirely her own fault and accusing her of stupidity. I protested at this and pointed out we had come to them for help and assistance not condemnation. There was little they could do legally, however, unless Evelyn was prepared to go and demand her passport back herself. She looked at me hopelessly. The sergeant confirmed that if I went along with Evelyn, there was more chance of getting the precious document returned. And if the loan sharks refused me, I could then come back to ask the police to accompany me.

Not quite knowing what I was getting myself into, I then headed for the "loan agency" with Evelyn, thinking there was no point in wasting time. This was a surreal experience, quite outside my normal expat life and that of any other expats I suspect.

The "bank," as it called itself, was at the heart of one of those large, labyrinthine, dark buildings which then stood, largely unnoticed, among the gleaming new monuments to wealth that made up Central Hong Kong's famous skyline. After negotiating several staircases and corridors we entered the main bank hall.

I was staggered. The scene that greeted me took my breath away. First, the size of the place was unexpected – about half a football pitch. Second, the sheer numbers of people was overwhelming. There must have been several hundred, perhaps three hundred Philippinas sitting dolefully in that hall, presumably live-in maids like Evelyn. Along the length of one side of the room ran the counters, protected by strong screen of wire mesh, behind which sat rows of tellers, also all female and Philippina, who dealt with their "customers" in lowered tones. An unpleasant hush pervaded the place – a hush of anxiety and fear.

My appearance caused a stir. Heads turned and whispering intensified. Europeans didn't come to a place like this. It boded trouble. A few women got up and left. Others averted their eyes as we sat down in the queue to one counter.

Finally, our turn came and we faced a middle-aged Philippina through the wire mesh, which reminded me of the visiting rooms of prisons. She was immediately hostile and launched into what I assumed was abuse of Evelyn in strident Tagalog. Evelyn hung her head, not knowing where to look.

I felt uncomfortable as the only foreigner there, but not threatened. I calculated, rightly or wrongly, that my being a foreigner was a protective factor. Interrupting her tirade I told her we had come to get Evelyn's passport back; that we demanded it be returned, now, and that holding it was illegal.

"She owes us money," the teller snapped back. "She gave us her passport as security. No-one forced her!"

"Fine," I replied, "but now she wants it back and you cannot hold it against her wishes."

Pushing her chair away roughly, the teller stood, turned away and went through a door behind her. I could see her talking quietly to an older Chinese man in the back room. Probably a Chinese-run operation, I thought, and possibly with triad connections.

She returned with the same message and began addressing Evelyn again. When I asked Evelyn what they were saying, she explained they were threatening her and her family in the Philippines.

At this I told the teller that we were not leaving until the passport was handed over and that if this was not done promptly I would fetch the police as I had already reported this case to them. I also said that measures would be taken to ensure that the loan would be dealt with. This bluff had the desired outcome, in that the woman disappeared again into the back room and after five minutes returned with Evelyn's passport. She aimed further insults to Evelyn as we rose and left. It was a relief to get out of there. All eyes followed us curiously as we left.

At least she had her passport and the means to visit her family that summer. Furthermore, we reduced her debt and she reluctantly agreed that a small amount should be kept back from her salary to repay a little more each month. And she swore she would not borrow more. Were we being paternalistic and helpful? Or were we just patronising expat employers on whom she was unwillingly dependent?

Life settled back into domestic routine, with no more disturbing phone calls or crises. After a couple of months, however, another problem arose. We noticed that our phone bills were soaring and found out that it was from the use of Evelyn's personal line, which we had installed for her.

It transpired that she was making regular calls to the United States. We were surprised to learn from Evelyn that she now had a boyfriend in the US. They had come in to contact via postal dating, and it was serious she assured us. Instinctively, we warned her about this. How could she know this man? What was his background? How could this work? She had never met him.

For her, it represented a lifeline. Like other Philippinas, a relationship or marriage to a foreigner meant escape from the poverty of home, or a release from the legal entrapment of working in Hong Kong. It could mean the chance for love and happiness. She persisted with this long distance affair, and a month or so later, to our great surprise, and disappointment at losing our faithful home help of five years, she announced that she was returning to the Philippines to meet her American admirer John. They were to be married and planned to live in the United States.

We parted friends, with tears and a feeling of genuine family loss. Our sadness was mitigated to some extent, however, by the knowledge that we were able to visit Evelyn in Manila a few months later. Coincidentally, we had been invited to visit the capital by a German friend who worked for the World Health Organisation. It was agreed we would visit Evelyn at her family home and the following Christmas we flew out to Manila.

Our hosts lived in the luxurious Manila suburb of Alabang, once home of the dictator Marcos and now a gated community for the wealthy elite and expats, thirteen miles from the city centre. With its swimming pools, manicured lawns, tennis clubs, large villa homes and armies of servants and guards, it was a world apart from the colourful, teeming, chaotic and in many parts, desperately poor city with which it was connected.

After a few days celebrating Christmas with our hosts in the microcosm of Alabang, we set out in their four-by-four to visit Evelyn. The journey was an eye-opener. Not that I was a newcomer to Manila. I had visited a few times as a tourist, but without seeing some of the areas we now drove through. Most were poor but not stricken. They seemed lively, noisy and full of life. But the shanty towns in the outer reaches were heart-wrenching. Built on mud flats and open sewers, they comprised of skeletal wooden shacks on posts, linked by rickety walkways. The stink was all pervading and the ragged nature of the children obvious.

Our six-year-old daughter was shocked at the scene, asking why these people were so poor. Our host, a doctor trying to lead mass inoculation campaigns for children throughout the Philippines, railed against the highly conservative and all powerful Catholic church, which preached against birth control of all kinds.

Finally, we left the city outskirts and headed for Evelyn's village. The arrival of a large ostentatious car, filled with foreigners, caused quite a stir in the village and we were quickly surrounded by delighted chattering children. Simple and scruffy, the village was welcoming and clean – quite unlike the slums we had passed through. Children were healthy looking and well clothed.

Evelyn greeted us self-consciously at her family home – a simple two storey concrete cottage, with linoleum floor and sparse furniture. Her mother and father were also reserved but friendly, offering us sweets and snacks. The brother, the drug addict, hung about at the back of the room and never spoke. Then we were introduced to John, Evelyn's fiancé, a burly and red-faced ex-GI, with standard close-cropped hair, who greeted us warmly. He seemed affable, kind and gentle. Perhaps Evelyn had struck lucky and her future would be secured.

We spent an hour with Evelyn and her family, chatting about Hong Kong and the past, without mentioning anything potentially embarrassing. Then we took Evelyn and John for a farewell meal at a local restaurant, before taking our leave. They seemed comfortable and happy together as we left. It was the last time we were to see her or hear from her.

Evelyn's successor in our family was Marjorie Cadienza, who we had met through Evelyn. Confident, organised, bustling, a good cook and financially astute, Marjorie was a complete contrast to Evelyn. She worked with us for a further ten years until we left Hong Kong in 2000.

Occasionally, she received news of Evelyn. It turned out Evelyn had been more than HK$60,000 in debt, rather than the HK$16,000 she admitted to us. A good portion of this had been loaned from friends as well as loan sharks. I learned from police friends that the loan sharks in Hong Kong were indeed triad run. If Philippinas did run away back home without paying their debts, the triads' reach extended that far and their families were in danger.

We also heard some years later that Evelyn and John had divorced and that Evelyn was living somewhere in the USA with her daughter. Let's hope she found some peace and independence.

Miss Hong Kong

By the time I came to enter the Miss Hong Kong Competition, I was already quite a seasoned expatriate, having worked and lived in the colony for almost twenty years. In 1996 it was still technically a British colony, but out of respect for the future we tended to call it a "territory" – that is, anticipating its coming status as a "Special Administrative Zone" of the People's Republic of China.

When I say I entered, I mean "we" entered – we being my secretary at the time, Charmaine Kung, and me, as prime sponsor. I hadn't until then had much to do with the showbiz side of Chinese life in Hong Kong. Although in possession of a rudimentary smattering of Cantonese, far more than most fellow expats I was proud to boast, I didn't understand enough to follow Cantonese TV.

I was aware that Miss Hong Kong was a major item on the annual calendar of ostentatious, noisy and kitschy Cantonese popular TV spectaculars. It probably ranked right up there with Hong Kong Horse of the Year Award, but I couldn't claim to be an aficionado and didn't know much about it.

Naturally, then, I was slightly surprised when the highly capable, cheerful Charmaine requested a confidential meeting at the end of an unmemorable working day. She closed my office door. Her serious and determined demeanour seemed to presage a resignation or salary increase request. But no.

"Frank, I want to ask you to do me a favour," she began, conspiratorially lowering her voice, and glancing suspiciously over her shoulder. Relieved, because Charmaine was proving to be a real help in our small PR business, I assured her of my willingness to grant any reasonable favour, thinking at the same time that this wouldn't include lending large sums of money to her.

"I'm entering Miss Hong Kong," she then announced regally, tossing her head coquettishly. "And I should like you to be my sponsor." She said this in a tone which strongly suggested she regarded this as a favour to me rather than the other way round.

Being a sensitive person, and genuinely liking Charmaine, I suppressed the urge to laugh. She was a pleasant looking young woman, always well groomed and with a cheerful disposition, but I couldn't really imagine her as a serious runner in a beauty contest. She was, to put it delicately, sturdy with a rounded figure, not lacking curves, but possessing rather too many with a round face. She had an infectious broad smile, luxuriant well-groomed hair, perfect teeth and a healthy, pink complexion. However, I didn't feel this was sufficient to put her in contention with some of that sophisticated city's beauties I constantly and discretely admired.

"Well, of course," I replied, trying to sound enthusiastic. "What do I have to do?"

"Don't worry," she grinned, "You don't have to pay anything – just sign this form. It's a formality." That was a relief, I must admit, because the thought of having to put down a deposit on Charmaine's chances of fame and fortune in the world of beauty would have been like betting on a workhorse winning the Grand National.

I still felt uneasy. I was discomforted by the thought of Charmaine being made to look foolish. Was I encouraging a flight of fancy that may see her humiliated? Should I be honest and forthright and discourage her? Perhaps that would be equally or more unkind. Better to show my support. I rationalised that she deserved my backing and confidence that she was a worthy entrant. However, I also retained a sneaking hope that it would all come to nothing. There was also the nagging thought that I might appear foolish too.

"By the way," Charmaine added on leaving my office, "Don't say anything to the others. I would like to keep this confidential." To my shame, I was relieved to hear this.

Several weeks rolled by, with the fast pace of the Hong Kong PR world occupying us all in the office. I was particularly busy, as we were trying to establish new offices in both Beijing and Singapore – efforts which ultimately proved fruitless, thanks to the Asian financial tsunami which swept over us in 1998. Thoughts of Miss Hong Kong and Charmaine's approach to me had faded away.

Then one Monday, at the end of office hours, as we finished some mundane office administration, she turned before going out of my office.

"Are you alright to come on Friday evening then?" she asked casually.

"Sorry, what's that for Charmaine?" I replied with unaffected innocence.

"The Miss Hong Kong competition of course, it starts on Friday!" she rejoined, with more than a hint of impatience.

My heart sank and I probably blushed. Images rushed through my mind of a bevy of slim, long-legged pretty Cantonese girls on a gaudily lit TV stage, with their suave sponsors by their side, while Charmaine and I stuck out like a couple of oddball hicks. I could see sideways glances and hear snide comments from the other contestants and the judges. I was already feeling like a rabbit in the headlights and I distinctly felt the soul-baring stare of the cameras. She pulled me abruptly from my reverie.

"We've got to be at the TVB studios in Sai Kung at 6:00 pm, so if you don't mind I ordered a taxi to pick you up here at the office after work. I'll be in the taxi because it's picking me up from the beauticians first. By the way, I'm sure you won't mind if I take Friday off. I've got a lot to do, obviously. You know, manicure, facial, hair, make-up, dressing – that sort of thing. Oh, you men, you don't really understand, do you?" she explained with firm authority.

"Right, but…erm…why are we going to the TV studios? And…um…why do I have to go?" I stammered. I thought I had done my bit by signing the form. I was wrong.

"First round photos and interviews," Charmaine beamingly pronounced. "You must accompany me as my sponsor."

I relaxed. Clearly this was just a kind of escort-chaperone role. Easy!

"Yes!" continued Charmaine, with growing enthusiasm. "We have an interview with the judges." I stiffened as my inner alarm system was triggered again.

"What do you mean "WE"?" I gulped.

"Of course, the judges have to ask the candidate and the sponsor questions to see if we are a serious participant," she clarified with a condescending air. "By the way, you have to tell them you've known me for at least five years."

Clearly, her boss, whom I think she respected in his business field, was rather dim when it came to beauty contests and Miss Hong Kong in particular.

"Good night!" she said breezily, and waltzed out.

A number of questions ran like ticker tape through my mind. Should I compromise my better judgement and go through with this? Should I have to appear on TV? Could I possibly let the enthusiastic, self-confident Charmaine down? What would the judges ask me? Could I lie to promote her entry? Yes – she's a beautiful girl! Yes – I think she should be Miss Hong Kong! Yes – she would make a wonderful Hong Kong entry into Miss Asia! But at the end of it all, I know full well that I had to go through with this and that I couldn't let my likeable secretary down. I resigned myself to the situation with an audible sigh.

Finally, Friday came around, and the office was buzzing with excitement. Of course, by then the rest of the staff were fully aware of Charmaine's bid for fame. I couldn't really make out from either my Chinese or European staffers whether they were simply amused by the whole affair, or whether they really shared in Charmaine's genuine belief in her destiny. Probably a measure of both.

Charmaine, as agreed, did not appear at work, in order to complete her lengthy preparations. I shuffled my way through the day, trying to concentrate on press releases and proposals. My wife, wickedly enjoying my discomfort with the whole affair, called me several times to revel in my uncertainty.

"Looking forward to seeing you on TV tonight, darling!" she teased.

Finally, at five o'clock, a good hour before her due arrival time to pick me up, a cacophony of cheers and gasps erupted in the main office. Charmaine had appeared in all her glory, just to give her fellow workers a glimpse of her majestic presence.

When I went out to join in the general admiration I was stunned by the apparition before me. My ordinary and slightly dumpy secretary appeared before me resembling something like a figure in a Beijing opera. Her hair was permed, puffed up, lacquered and set with waves and curls. It shone like glistening coal.

Her face was made up like a puppet, with lavish, green-brown eye shadow and dark liner; and blood red rouge lipstick, which contrasted like a gash on her heavily powdered and chalky cheeks, lightly rouged so that they resembled a couple of Granny Smith apples.

She wore a very tight fitting long cheong-sam, the favoured and flattering tradition formal wear of the Chinese woman. Charmaine's was bright red, flecked with gold braiding and appliqués. It was indeed a transformation, and whatever I thought of the effect on her chances, I had to respect her chutzpah and determination. She was going to make her mark!

After much cooing, gasping, giggling and aiyyee-ahs from the girls in the office, we made our way out. Charmaine was serene. She glided rather than walked. She turned her head aristocratically away from the bemused looks of the other office workers in the lift. She deigned to allow me to open doors for her, nodding her appreciation as if to a junior footman.

The taxi ride to the TVB studios was lengthy and uncomfortable. As usual the Friday night traffic was horrendous, with long queues before the famous Hong Kong Cross Harbour Tunnel and the predictable noise and congestion being quite wearisome.

During the ride Charmaine sat elegantly and proudly, confidently telling me of her plans for the future.

"Of course, if I win, I shall have to take a year off, and you'll need to find a replacement," she informed me. "Don't worry though, I'll help you recruit a good person to help."

"Miss Hong Kong has many duties and I expect I shall have to travel quite a lot. She has to open events and appear on TV shows, and represent Hong Kong at many overseas functions," she continued.

I was taken aback by the change from the conditional to the future tense and the intermitted use of the first and third person singular. This lady really thought she had a good chance.

"Well, we would certainly miss you, Charmaine!" I said, weakly.

"I know, but don't worry." She leaned over and patted me on the shoulder. "I'll make sure that you get my PR contract."

"And also, you can be sure that I won't become the mistress of any tycoons!" she added defiantly.

It was indeed a constant rumour that various former Miss Hong Kongs had been the kept women of certain very wealthy Hong Kong Chinese businessmen. How much of this was true, I have no idea, but the scurrilous Hong Kong Chinese showbiz media revelled in such innuendo and the truth of the matter, as usual with the media, was not allowed to get in the way.

"What do you think they will ask us about?" I asked tentatively.

"Oh, just normal things – like how you know me and our backgrounds, what kind of music and clothes you like…and what you like in girls maybe!!" she giggled.

I didn't fancy the way things were developing.

"And is this interview live on TV?" I ventured.

"Yes, should be," she replied, "Especially as you are a gweilo!"

This was a bit shocking. "Gweilo" was simply a slang Cantonese word for foreigner. Actually it means "white devil" and was once quite insulting. But these days most gweilos used the term themselves in a light-hearted way. No, I wasn't concerned about being labelled a gweilo. What concerned me was the sudden thought that I might be something of an exception in this very Chinese showbiz occasion, and therefore the object of particular curiosity. It crossed my mind that this very fact was a part of the cunning strategy of my protégé.

Nor was I phased by appearing on TV per se. I had done my part professionally for clients, in front of the cameras, as a fairly experienced PR man by that time. But the thought of being on Chinese TV, as a kind of freak, talking about fashion and beauty and showbiz – all subjects in which I was largely ignorant – filled me with trepidation. I needed to be properly briefed and prepared. I needed to know something about the subjects I was going to be publicly quizzed about. I was beginning to perspire.

Finally we drew near the TVB studios. TVB was one of two available stations at that time in Hong Kong. Both had English and Chinese channels. The English channels were under-funded on account of their limited viewing audience and therefore reduced advertising appeal. They were generally mediocre, purveying a regular stream of second hand US and UK sitcoms and dramas. However, they did school some individually talented young Chinese and western journalists, who managed to put out some decent news and sports programmes.

The Chinese channels, on the other hand, commanded huge audiences and budgets. They made good money for their tycoon owners. Hong Hong's population of over six million were avid viewers and they revelled in colourful, noisy soaps, Cantonese pop specials, dramas and spectaculars – like Miss Hong Kong. The more garish, the more fun, the more outlandishly extravagant, the better.

My time was approaching. As we turned into the drive, leading down the main entrance, I was telling myself that this would be interesting, fun and that I had nothing to worry about.

At that point, I noticed ahead of us some thirty yards, a great throng of photojournalists and cameramen – possibly 40 or 50 of them. Charmaine noticed this too, and as I shrank back into the dark recesses of the taxi, she began to swell up like a peacock.

As we pulled up the throng crowded around our taxi, blinding us with flash photography and dazzling TV camera lights. Charmaine was in heaven. She grabbed my hand.

"Come on, you have to escort me," she ordered.

I pushed the photographers and cameras back as we cautiously emerged, finding just enough room on the pavement to stand. Microphones and tape recorders were shoved under our noses.

At first the questions were a meaningless jumble of Cantonese quick fire questions, aimed naturally at Charmaine. As she pouted and posed, fluttered her eyelashes and tossed back her hair with film star style, I noticed that she was beginning to refer to me. She held on to my arm as her escort.

Then it was my turn.

"Mr Wiggie, how long you know Miss Kung?"

"Mr Wing Gay, how long you live Hong Kong?"

"Mr Fan Wing, why you like Miss Kung?"

"Mr Wung Kee, you love Miss Kung?"

"Miss Kung your girlfriend?"

"Mr Fan, you think Miss Kung very beautiful?"

"Mr Fat Wan, you thing Miss Kung win Miss Hong Kong?"

The enquiries came thick and fast. I summoned up every last piece of PR technique I had so often intoned to clients. I stayed cool. I concentrated on one question at a time. I looked the questioner in the eye. I smiled. Internally I was a bag of nerves. Presumably, this was being beamed live on Chinese TV and radio, or at least recorded. I was afraid of making a fool of myself.

However, the Chinese media are enthusiastic, not unscrupulous, like some UK press. They are generally courteous, if over exuberant. I was used to my name being mispronounced. Wingate is a bit of a mouthful to a Cantonese speaker, who in his or her native tongue is not accustomed to stringing consecutive consonants together. So after a while, when I realised that the questioning was light-hearted and harmless, my ego awoke and I started to enjoy myself.

Gradually, we made our way, with the scrum around us gradually dissipating, to the studio door, until we slipped inside and finally escaped.

Once inside, we were shown to the waiting area, which was a shabby corridor with a line of plastic chairs along the wall. In fact the whole studio interior was disappointingly unglamorous – as, I subsequently learnt, all TV studios are – apart from the sets themselves which appear on camera.

The place was full of applicants. Good-looking, highly made-up young Chinese girls, with their escorts or sponsors, who ranged, it seemed, from Grandma to boyfriend. Looking around confirmed to me that Charmaine was indeed a long odds outsider. I was also very aware that I was the only European face among the 50 or 60 people gathered there. We certainly elicited some strange looks and curious glances. I felt conscious that some of the others might consider me to be some kind of "sugar daddy". Meanwhile, Charmaine unselfconsciously clung on to my arm and beamed with satisfaction. She did admit she was a little nervous.

Finally, our time came, and we were summoned by a very smart, rather officious young lady, who called out our names in Cantonese and ticked them off on a clipboard. We followed her into a cavernous and gloomy studio. Set in the centre was a long desk, behind which sat the three interviewers. Before them, two plastic chairs for us. Two or three cameras with glaring lights were set around the scene.

Our hosts greeted us cordially and explained that the interview would be filmed, but was not live, and may be used later if Charmaine progressed in the competition. That was a relief anyway and I relaxed.

There were three interviewers. The first, who greeted us, was the lady who had called us in. I guessed she was an up-and-coming junior executive from her manner, which seemed designed to impress the other two. The second, a handsome young man, with spiky, punky sort of hair, was fashionably dressed and affected an air of boredom and indifference through the whole thing. He did eye me curiously I noticed. I put him down as a Cantonese TV star of some kind. Indeed, Charmaine told me later, he was to be the host for the final, televised round.

Finally, a more mature Chinese gentleman, with a distinguished greying full head of hair, elegantly but casually dressed, led the interview. I assumed he was the director or producer.

Most questions were put to Charmaine in Cantonese. I understood a little and could see that they were not particularly penetrating. She responded breathlessly and excitedly, revelling in the occasion and enjoying being centre of attention.

Turning to me the senior interviewer addressed me in faultless English.

"Mr Wingate, thank you for joining us today. It's very unusual to have a Westerner participate. What made you think of nominating Miss Kung?"

I explained that Charmaine was my secretary and how she has approached me and that I thought she had a lot of personality and was very popular and that I thought she should enter.

The younger panellist whispered something, unsmilingly, to the elder statesman.

"Mr Yeung wonders what special characteristics of beauty and grace you consider Miss Kung possesses that you think she could be Miss Hong Kong."

This was a bit below the belt. I determined to face this out, not only for my sake but to give Charmaine "face".

"She's a very smart and attractive person," I said. "She deals with her colleagues and our clients with charm and ability. She's confident and capable in public situations."

I thought this was reasonable compromise between not supporting her enough and sounding falsely optimistic.

And so the interview continued for a few more minutes.

How long had I been in Hong Kong? What did I do for a job? Did I like Hong Kong? Was I familiar with Miss Hong Kong? Nothing particularly difficult.

When we had finished and were outside again, Charmaine told me she was going for a celebratory dinner with her family, so I should find myself a taxi to head home. She was glowing at this stage, very grateful to me, and enjoying a moment of triumph. I could sense she was proud that she had gone through it all, which must have been something of an ordeal for her too.

The following week the office was brimming with anticipation. The rest of the team had indeed seen Charmaine and myself on Chinese TV news, in a short clip about this year's entrants to Miss Hong Kong. They were keen to know all the details about our adventure. Charmaine dealt with all the questions with an imperious self-confidence, being slightly condescending about the arrangements, I noticed. She had certainly raised her status among the staff for having gone through with it all.

Predictably, she never progressed. A week later, she received notice that she hadn't been selected to go through to the next round. To my surprise she exhibited no disappointment at all. Amid expressions of consolation from us all, she shrugged her shoulders and dismissed the matter, before getting back to work. We never really spoke about it much afterwards.

Charmaine continued to work with me for the next five years, until I left Hong Kong. We had an informal, good-humoured and highly effective working relationship. I feel she benefited from the experience, gaining in confidence and poise. Although it caused me some doubts initially, I thought, in retrospect, they were completely unnecessary.

Instead I think of her bid with admiration. Why not have a go? We both had some fun because of her determination to take part. There was something typically Hong Kong in the affair – the corny razzamatazz, the exuberance, the lack of self-consciousness, the unbounded optimism and sense of fun.

Whenever I see a reference to Miss Hong Kong, or indeed Miss Anywhere, I can't help thinking of Charmaine and chuckling to myself.

Flirting with Cantonese

When I arrived in Hong Kong at the very end of 1977, I knew nothing about the Cantonese language. In fact, I knew very little about the Cantonese. This didn't really seem to matter, because Hong Kong was a British colony and the official language was English. Working life was conducted mainly in English and most Hong Kong people under 50 years old had learnt some, so everyday life was easy too.

Not much motivation to learn Cantonese then. That was certainly the view of the vast majority of expats, for whom this ancient language was entirely alien and much too difficult to learn. There was a degree of truth in this. Cantonese is certainly strange to the European ear at first, having no connections of sound, rhythm or vocabulary with the Indo-European family. Above all, the tonal basis of the language, where the very meaning of homonyms depends on the pitch with which it is uttered, made the task of acquiring it appear nigh impossible.

Nevertheless, there was also an element of colonial laziness, even arrogance, behind the widespread expat reluctance to learn. After all, wasn't learning the local language – unless you were a diplomat or a policeman – slightly patronising, like "going native"? Wasn't it "insincere" to learn a tongue with limited application in the world?

First impressions of Cantonese were bewildering. It was hard over the first few months to detect any patterns at all. Being monosyllabic, with each syllable beginning with a consonant followed by an open vowel, it sounded like verbal anti-aircraft ack-ack, rhythmic, loud and usually very fast.

This verbal structure meant that Cantonese speakers, in learning English, found it challenging to string consonants together. For example, my first address in Hong Kong was Stubbs Road, named after a long forgotten governor. In Cantonese, this broke up into "See-toe-but" Road. My English lady hostess corrupted it differently, calling it "Sir Tubsy" Road. I also learnt early on that my name, Frank, converted into "Fat Lan", as in the world famous crooner Fat-lan-see-nah-di-lah (Sinatra).

Chinese drivers of the subway trains were, in the early days of the system, tortured into announcing the stations' names in English as well as Cantonese. One, famously quoted among my friends, would come out regularly with "Plinks Awah", a valiant attempt at the Prince Edward stop in Kowloon.

It seemed like everyone was arguing all the time! And every sentence appeared to end with an "Aaaaah" conclusion, whether forceful, irritated, questioning or reassuring, depending on the cadence. Often they ended in "Aiiieeyah!" – a summative declaration meaning anything from "Oh no!" to "Well I never!" or even "Ouch!"

Nevertheless, I was keen to learn some Cantonese. I was encouraged by British colleagues of a similar age, also embarking on their Hong Kong adventure by joining the Royal Hong Kong Police Force. They were put through six months of intensive Cantonese, and some of them emerged very successfully fluent. One of their first steps was to learn a song. Sung to the tune of Camptown Races, it went:

"Jo san, gweilo, lei ho ma? Gei ho, gei ho.

Jo san gweilo, lei ho ma? Gei ho, lei ho ma?"

It meant "Good morning gweilo (foreigner) how are you? Quite well! Quite well! Good morning gweilo, how are you? Quite well, how are you?"

I bought myself a dense Cantonese primer. It had not been revised much from the time it was written – in the early fifties at the time of the Korean War. Using a Romanised spelling system, called the Wade-Giles system, it presented a grammar based step by step approach. I think it was produced by the CIA to deter people from learning a potentially subversive language at a time of intense US-Chinese hostility. To call it challenging would be a compliment.

If my formal language learning efforts made glacial progress, however, my interest in everyday Cantonese was greatly stimulated by the circumstances of my first job in Hong Kong – teaching English at the famous St Paul's Boys School. Here I taught local boys from eleven to eighteen years old. As one of only two non-Chinese on the staff (the other was the American deputy head) I was warmly welcomed by the other teachers. St. Paul's was an English medium school, so all the staff spoke English, though the staff room language of relaxation was naturally Cantonese and I began to pick up the odd word or common phrase.

Classroom teaching was a delight. The students were diligent and polite. My teaching apprenticeship in Yorkshire, dealing with decent but noisy and impudent coalminers' sons, was a torture in comparison.

At St. Paul's all students stood up when the teacher entered the room and would recite, in Cantonese, "Good Morning Teacher!" or "Good Afternoon!" in unison, with rather weary enthusiasm. They sat in uniform rows – at least forty of them in each class – and my first Cantonese challenge was to learn their names and pronounce them accurately.

To help all teachers, the names of all the boys were typed onto a classroom plan sellotaped onto the teacher's desk.

Cantonese names are invariably of three syllables – the first being the family name. Thus Wong Wing Cheung was from the Wong family. The boys would call each other by their family name, with a familiar "Ah" stuck at the front. Wong Wing Cheung therefore became "Ah-Wong" – something like in English calling someone named Smith "Smithy".

It was puzzling at first to get to grips with all these strange names. Some sounded funny to the English ear, like "Wun Big Tat" or "Pong Chau Fat" and I could remember them better, but others took time.

Although very polite, the boys were still mischievous and had an enormous amount of fun at my expense with their Cantonese jokes.

After I had been there for a few weeks, and had just gone into the classroom, I received the usual warm morning greeting from the standing boys. This was followed by some stifled giggles and muffled comments as they sat down. But this time, quite suddenly, one of my Cantonese colleagues marched through the open door and berated the class angrily. On finishing, he turned to me, apologised, and left, leaving me puzzled in an embarrassed silence and a class of shamefaced students.

At the next break, he came up to me and explained the incident. Those boys, he said, had been very cheeky, saying "Jo san, lo su!" to me for "Good morning, Sir!", when they should have been chanting "Jo san, lo si!" "Lo si" means "sir", but "lo su" means "rat".

One of the classes was also responsible for finding me a humorous Cantonese nickname, which stuck with me all my subsequent years in Hong Kong. Some things, like teachers' nicknames, are the same in classrooms the world over.

Transliterating the syllables Frank Win Gate into Cantonese, they came up with Fat Wan Gai, which literally means "dizzy" or "poxy" chicken. I preferred the more genteel "Fan Wing Gay" which means "everlasting foundation", but somehow it was never adopted by Cantonese friends.

As time moved on, of course, Hong Kong's vernacular became more familiar to the ear and the daily necessities required some effort to speak it. Moving around, for example, meant that I picked up place names in Cantonese and acquired a simple formula for engaging with cab drivers, most of whom didn't speak English. Thus "Pow-ma-day" or, literally "Run Horse Place" for Happy Valley, famous for its race course, or "Boon-san-kooi", "Half Mountain District" or Mid-levels, soon rolled off the tongue.

This basic knowledge was all relatively simple, but for non-Chinese friends sounded terribly impressive. The well-rehearsed Cantonese dialogue with cab drivers followed a routine pattern. "Where to?" "Happy Valley, please". "Oh, you speak Cantonese?" (Cab drivers were constantly amazed any foreigners spoke any Cantonese, or at least feigned surprise out of politeness) "No, only a little". "No, you speak really well. Do you live here?" "Yes, I've been here four years". "Where are you from?" "England". "Do you like Hong Kong?" "Yes, I've many friends here", and so on.

My German girlfriend at the time, later my wife, considered this to be remarkable fluency in Cantonese and added to my intellectual stock and sex appeal. Naturally I didn't own up to the fact that beyond the set five or six phrases of this ritualistic conversation I was lost and didn't understand a word if the subject matter deviated in the slightest from the set phrases.

Food offered a similar motivation for learning and speaking and the rich variety of Chinese cuisine provided a new world of vocabulary. Unfortunately, for the English speaker's ear, anyway, the Cantonese word for eating is "sick". At least it followed on logically that "sick-faan", or "eat-rice" is dinner or meal; and "ho-sick" or "good-eat" is delicious; and "sick-yin" or "eat-smoke" is smoking.

You soon learnt your favourite dishes, such as dim sum variants. "Ha gau" – prawn dumpling – and "siu mai" – pork balls – for example, were common expat favourites. Less popular but one dish I came to enjoy was "fong zhau". This literally means "phoenix claws" but actually they are chickens' feet. Eating fong zhau was beyond most expats but a sure way to demonstrate to Cantonese friends that you were either a veteran or at any rate an OK sort of person.

Ordering, however, needed care to avoid embarrassment. Cantonese's tonal nuances meant that mistakes were easy. I remember in one restaurant causing great hilarity among my Chinese friends, as well as the waiter, by over-confidently ordering "Guy-see-faan" which should mean "Chicken strips on rice". Unfortunately, by getting the tone of the second syllable slightly wrong, I had called for "chicken shit on rice."

Much safer, then, to go for "sau-see-guy" or "hand stripped chicken", which is a whole chicken, steamed for a couple of hours, then torn apart by hand and drenched in a soy, garlic and ginger sauce. Definitely "ho sick". Better not consume it with too much rice, though, otherwise you will be considered greedy, and you might be dubbed a "faan tung" or "rice bucket" by your Cantonese friends.

If hunger encouraged language inquisitiveness, sex was an even stronger impulse to master some flattering phrases. What better way to impress a Hong Kong girl than to demonstrate your expertise in her own tongue? However, this had to take into account the essentially down-to-earth nature of Cantonese when it came to sweet-talking.

For example, you won't find any endearments in the local tongue. I tried in vain to discover the equivalents of "Darling" or "Sweetheart" or "Dearest", but there are none. That's not to say in the least that Cantonese girls are any less romantic or passionate, but these feelings are not expressed directly. For Chinese girls actions speak louder than words.

Even saying "I love you" doesn't sound romantic in Cantonese, certainly not to the European ear, anyway. "Gnaw-oi-lay" comes across rather more like a type of mineral. Then again, the common word in Hong Kong for husband is "lo gung", which directly translated means "old man" as in the English slang, "my ol' man". Wife, similarly, is "lo por" – "old woman". Hence, a "lo por lo" is an "old woman slave" or a hen-pecked husband.

But this lack of apparent romanticism did not stop us single beaus optimistically flirting, armed with our limited vocabulary. We could learn to say "ney-ho-leng-nui", for example, meaning you are a very beautiful girl, though that often produced a response like "yow-mo-gow-chaw" (basically, "you must be joking"!). It was important not to get the response "ham-sap-lo" which accused you of being a "salty wet man". In others words a dirty old man or a lecher. Equally negative was "woo dip" as a response, as this labelled you a butterfly or a flirt, and not to be taken at all seriously.

After some years in Hong Kong I decided to make more of an effort to learn Chinese, but I opted for Mandarin, as it seemed to represent the future. Most Hong Kong Chinese were paying more attention to the national language, with the gradual approach of 1997 and the handover to China.

I have to admit my motives weren't purely linguistic. There was a young woman involved. I had met Nicky Wong a couple of years previously and when our paths crossed again I was quite struck by her. Fluent in English, she was pretty, well-educated and fun.

I tried to establish a relationship with her, but met with little success. Whilst we had some enjoyable dates, she resisted any kind of consistency, on the grounds that her family was very conservative and being involved with a foreigner would not be acceptable. This, she explained with convincing sincerity, was not a matter of racism, or even cultural bias, but a problem about communication. How could she become committed to someone who spoke no Cantonese, or even Mandarin and couldn't even hold a conversation with her family?

This sounded reasonable and contributed to my idea to study Mandarin, or Putonghua, the national dialect or "common language". My aim was to learn simple everyday conversation and to be able to read the newspaper. And to impress Nicky. I wanted to learn to read simplified characters, those devised by the communist regime to enable people to become literate more easily. I understood I would need a minimum of four thousand characters to attain the desired standard. In Hong Kong the traditional complex characters were still in use, as in Taiwan, but most people could read simplified as well.

Rather than study on a formal course, which would have been difficult, given the long and erratic hours that my job at that time demanded, I planned to teach myself with the aid of a good textbook and a fluent speaker to coach me. To this end I found Hazel Cheung, a friend of a friend, who was a Hong Kong girl and a native level Putonghua speaker.

It was an inventive arrangement. Hazel would come to my flat twice a week for an hour. With my teaching background I conducted the lesson following the exercises in the book, while Hazel corrected my pronunciation and intonation! In return, I paid Hazel by allowing her to occupy my flat for two hours a week to practise her erhu playing. The erhu is the traditional Chinese two string violin and the problem I was solving for Hazel was that her father forbad her to practise at home. Perhaps she wasn't very good at it. I don't know. I was never there when she played.

And so my foray into Mandarin was launched. It began with several monotonous weeks of reciting tones. Hazel was not as compliant a teacher as I expected and proved quite bossy. She would not let me progress until I had mastered the four basic tones of Putonghua.

"Ma" – flat high tone. "Ma" – rising tone, as if asking a question – ma? "Ma" low looping tone, as if asking a question uncertainly. "Ma" falling tone, as if affirming a point at the end of a sentence. It seemed ridiculous to me at first. But it was absolutely necessary, as each "Ma" meant something completely different. It could mean "Mum" "Horse" "Grasshopper" or "Toad", depending on the tone. And, of course, you have to remember, I was only being drilled in four tones, whereas Cantonese demanded at least nine!

I never became too obsessed about learning Putonghua, treating it like an enjoyable hobby rather than a duty, and using it to play around with Cantonese friends, with whom I would adopt a mock superiority as speaking their "national" language occasionally better than them.

Slowly but patiently I worked my way through that primer for two years, even doing an amount of homework in between lessons, and completed what might be called an introductory course – basic conversation. At the end of that period I could also recognise about a thousand characters and began to identify patterns in the script – though still at a level of little practical application.

Putonghua differs mainly from Cantonese in pronunciation. Most Hong Kong people could understand Putonghua speakers, but the understanding wasn't normally reciprocated, as Cantonese, particularly in Hong Kong, was full of contemporary urban slang and humour which mainlanders couldn't necessarily decipher.

Putonghua speakers considered themselves to be holding the moral high ground, being exponents of the official language of national unity. For some scholars Cantonese was a vulgar southern dialect, lacking finesse. Hadn't it been said that a Cantonese love song sounded like a bar room brawl? Could we compare the stand-off with received English as against a broad Cockney accent? Or perhaps High German with some Swiss German cantonal versions?

The Cantonese countered this by claiming history was on their side. Cantonese, it was argued, was the authentic, original Chinese language, which survived in the South, whereas Mandarin, and then Putonghua, was a mongrel dialect corrupted by the non-Han language of the invading Mongol hordes fresh off the Siberian steppes.

The softer sounds of Putonghua made it somehow more attractive, with the sibilant "shsh" "sze" and "zh" consonants a gentler alternative to the harsher plosive Cantonese consonants. Eventually I became reasonable at pronunciation and even mastered the famous Putonghua tongue twister – "Forty-four stone lions".

Four is "si" with a falling tone. Ten is "shi" with a rising tone. So forty-four is "si-shi-si". Stone is "shi" – a rising tone, and lion is "shi" the high flat tone. So with a classifier that precedes the noun lion – "zhi" – and the diminutive "zi" at the end, the phrase reads "si-shi-si-zhi-shi-shi-zi". Not much help in everyday conversation, but mastery of this tongue twister impressed a few Chinese friends and is still a passable party piece at dinner parties back in the UK.

Although I was a leisure time and half-hearted student, who never reached a workable level of fluency, I did, however, very much enjoy learning the basics of the language, and it helped me understand much more about Cantonese. This was mainly because the grammar of both is almost identical and knowledge of Putonghua enabled me to better understand the sentence structure and phrasing of Cantonese.

It also demonstrated that the mental block many expats have in tackling Cantonese or Mandarin is largely unnecessary, for one major discovery about these tongues is that their grammar is uncomplicated compared to European versions. For example, as someone who had to battle with declining nouns, conjugating verbs, complex tenses and genders, in learning Latin and German, what a relief it was to discover that Chinese nouns and verbs have only one form; that tenses, as verb constructs, don't exist, and that normal nouns are not masculine, feminine or neuter!

Such complexities, learned Chinese friends assured me, are the encumbrances of relatively primitive language forms, whereas, in its six thousand year development, Chinese had rendered them superfluous and eventually, redundant.

Unfortunately, the flip side to this convenient grammatical and verbal simplification is the use of tones to distinguish meaning and intent. It is a bit of a struggle for the European to grasp that the word "gow" in Cantonese, for instance, can mean number nine, dog, dumpling, crescent shape, or prick (penis), depending on the tone.

Enormous fun provided here for your Cantonese friends, who revelled in the opportunity for punning these homonyms offered. How I remember it taking me a couple of years to realise that the term "sap-gow", which means "nineteen" spoken one way, can mean "wet-dick", or masturbation, if said with altered tones. Plenty of laughs there for my Hong Kong colleagues at work.

Another sexual joke revolved around the phrase "da-fay-gay". This could mean cigarette lighter (hit-fire-machine) when rendered with appropriate nuances. It could, however, also mean "shoot the aeroplane" or "shoot-fly-machine" with slightly different tones. Had to be careful here, though, because that was also slang for ejaculation. Furthermore, get it slightly wrong, as "da-four-gay" and you are striking the waiter.

It was inevitable to learn a few curses, particularly as I played soccer against Chinese opponents, who, like their expat brothers of the field, may be perfect gentlemen in normal life, but turn into foul-mouthed yobs once in the team strip and battling for the ball.

As in London slang, "fuck" was used often, but as a common enforcing adjective rather than such a bad word. The Cantonese "deeyu" seem softer than the English version, and is often used just for "oh, God!" or "Damn!" One could of course spice it up a little by extending it into "deeyu-lay-lo-mo!" which introduces mothers into the expression and when directed at an opponent could well provoke an untidy brawl.

It always amused me greatly to hear this swearword used by football crowds. Often at major local matches, up to eighty thousand fans would pack into the Hong Kong Stadium. Whenever someone missed an open goal or made a clumsy mistake it seemed like every single person in the crowd joined in concert to produce a collective "deeyu" like a great sigh to express their disappointment or disapproval.

As I've been back home some ten years now, the opportunities to practise Cantonese, or Putonghua, have narrowed. Naturally, I attempt to show off by ordering certain dishes at restaurants in Chinatown in London. However, this embarrasses my children and, more often than not, will be greeted by "Sorry mate, I don't speak Chinese" by the obviously ethnic Chinese waiter.

If I have a single regret about my enjoyable years in Hong Kong, it is that I didn't apply myself more seriously and systematically to learning Cantonese and Putonghua. There's nothing else I regret from a time in my life that was challenging, exotic, unpredictable and great fun.

Putonghua is probably slightly easier to learn than Cantonese, and has a wider global application in the coming years. Cantonese, however, is immensely colourful, evolving, mischievous and expressive.

More foreigners should learn it. There's no need to be deterred by the many tones. Learners should forget the tones, listen to friends and just imitate the phrasing. I reached a passable level of street wise Cantonese for shopping, travelling around, dining and having fun with Chinese friends. Making an effort was always appreciated, and, at the very least, caused sympathetic amusement. It always broke the ice, not least because the old colonial legacy meant few foreigners ever deigned to learn the common vernacular. That must have caused resentment!

I wished at the very least to be considered a "lek-jai", that is a smart boy, rather than a "gwy-daan" or a turtle's egg, meaning a dumb wit. Of, course, gwy-daan can also convey the sense of expensive egg with the right intonation.

There was another regret. I never did get as close as I would have liked to the lovely Nicky Wong. She couldn't contemplate a relationship with someone not intimate to her language and culture. Imagine my dismay then, when I learnt some years later, that she finished up marrying an Australian. Deeyu-lay-lo-mo!

Handover

In 1982, when Margaret Thatcher had her history-making confrontation with Deng Xiao-ping in Beijing over the future of Hong Kong – a meeting which sent a shiver of anxiety through the city – I was an expatriate of thirty something, single, and more interested in my love life and social agenda than the fate of Britain's last real colony.

That's not to say that I wasn't aware of increasing pressure on the British and Chinese governments to resolve the Hong Kong "problem". The clock was ticking and 1997, when the treaties governing the colony's status ran out, was drawing ever nearer. Long term investment and political decisions had to be made, and the topic dominated media, business and bar talk.

For us expats, of course, the question was partly academic. Whilst we might feel close attachment and genuine affection for the place, we had passports giving us the right to live elsewhere if the debate turned ugly. For the local Hong Kong Chinese, many of whom had fled from communism in the first place, the future was potentially dangerous and, at the least, deeply uncertain.

There were the diehard colonialists who believed that somehow Thatcher, basking in the Falklands war victory, would bluster her way with the Chinese leaders and keep Hong Kong British. She herself apparently thought this possible. There were those who imagined some sort of administrative compromise, enabling the Brits to administer Hong Kong, while surrendering sovereignty, was attainable. And there were the realists, who could see that the British negotiating position was very weak, and that China would be adamant in reversing what they saw, with considerable justification, was a historical injustice, forced upon them at a time of national weakness a century and a half earlier.

Thatcher found Deng immoveable. The tough old revolutionary, making regular use of his spittoon during the meeting, was in no mood for compromise. If the British wanted to be difficult, he told the British premier, we will just walk in and take Hong Kong and you won't be able to stop us. She retorted that China's reputation on the world stage would be damaged. He wasn't interested.

Technically, Britain had a legal right to rule the island of Hong Kong in perpetuity, but this was meaningless without the New Territories hinterland. Thatcher had to face reality. Hong Kong would become a "Special Administrative Zone" within China, with its own administration and institutions. This was Deng's famous "One Country – Two Systems" formula. The best of Hong Kong would be retained. It was, after all, a port, financial centre and investor of great significance. Why kill the layer of golden eggs?

A "Joint Declaration" was signed and a Joint Liaison Committee set up which afforded Britain token rights to ensure the terms of the agreement were adhered to.

Thatcher swept imperiously into Hong Kong and at a landmark press conference ensured the people of the territory that the UK had succeeded in protecting their future. Typically the local media were compliant – except one. A former BBC reporter, and then writer for the Far Eastern Economic Review, Emily Lau, challenged the Iron Lady. She questioned the morality of the UK government in handing over seven million Hong Kong people to a communist dictatorship.

How dare she question the Prime Minister? Thatcher brushed it aside. Lau must be the only person in Hong Kong who had a problem with the agreement, she insisted. But the challenge reverberated around the territory and Lau had touched a sensitive nerve.

So the die was cast and the years 1982-1989, on the back of the agreement being signed, witnessed a frenetic surge in economic development in both Hong Kong and China.

Hong Kong was transforming itself at breakneck speed from a low cost manufacturing centre into a managerial, design, marketing and financial entrepot of extraordinary wealth and power, belying its size and limitations. This was largely on the back of China opening up. After the Joint Agreement laid out a path, Hong Kong businesses, expat and Chinese alike, leapt at the opportunities that China's enormous reservoir of labour and cheap assets offered. "Made in Hong Kong" was rapidly turning into "Made by Hong Kong".

China, the giant which Napoleon famously said was best left slumbering, was now stirring – the economy being stimulated by the open door policy initiated by Deng. The country was lumbering down the very capitalist road that Mao had so passionately vilified, launching the anarchy of the cultural revolution in his effort to block that route.

Hong Kong entrepreneurs wasted no time in transporting whole factories into neighbouring Shenzhen, to take advantage of wage rates one fifteenth of Hong Kong's.

For many people, including myself, this was a period of opportunity and excitement. As well as the wealthy entrepreneurs, most expats and the fast-growing Chinese middle class enjoyed new job openings and rising living standards. My personal journey took me from school teaching to freelance writing and editing to public relations. I joined a fast-growing, creative PR company, run by a young Londoner, which specialised in sport, but quickly expanded into other areas. In five years it grew from five staff to forty, with new offices in Tokyo and Singapore.

It was a hard-working, but young environment, with long and asocial hours being balanced by partying and drinking, often with the journalists we catered to. In many ways it typified the attitude of many expats and better off Chinese. Life was good, so make money and enjoy your time, because the future was still uncertain.

It was distinctly more uncertain for those who didn't possess an alternative passport. During the eighties many Hong Kong Chinese sought to gain their "insurance" against the handover going sour. This meant getting out to Canada, or Australia, or Singapore; going to a safe haven, acquiring a passport and then, maybe, coming back to Hong Kong to enjoy the economic boom.

For many others this wasn't an option. They didn't have the necessary skills or capital to succeed in emigrating. For them, the safeguards against a capricious or unpredictable Chinese government could only be constitutional or legal. Voicing their concerns were democrats like Emily Lau, who turned to politics full time and Martin Lee, a well-spoken barrister. They argued coherently and passionately that the British Government owed it to the people of Hong Kong to ·grant them the right to settle in the UK, or leave them, at the very least, the protection of local representative government.

During the eighties, neither of these options were politically realistic. Thatcher was in no position to convince the British people that six million Hong Kong Chinese would be given the right to immigrate. At the same time, the idea of introducing democracy into the colony seemed opportunist, when neither the colonial power, nor the citizens, and certainly not the incoming sovereign power, had ever shown much interest in representative reform.

And so the eighties roared along, with most Hong Kongers making the most of the boom. It was a period of short term optimism and cautious hope for the future. Surely the Chinese Government, the new pragmatic "socialist market" regime, was too hard headed and too sensible to jeopardise the obvious benefits Hong Kong brought to China's economic renaissance? Surely the Chinese and British together would broker a practical transition administration which could maintain those elements of Hong Kong's success which had served it so well – open economy, free trade, free press, rule of law and relatively corrupt-free executive.

So while the protracted negotiations between British and Chinese governments about the nature of post-handover structures and the form of handover ceremonies ground on in the background, most of us focussed on the present and didn't think of the political changes ahead.

Meanwhile, Hong Kong society was changing. With growing wealth, a self-confident Chinese middle class was asserting itself. Simultaneously outdated colonial assumptions of superiority were fast disappearing. Foreigners and Chinese socialised, dated and married freely. They worked together on equal terms. Young Chinese were returning from top US, Canadian, British and Australian universities, confident, well educated, multi-lingual and international in outlook, ready to take over the pinnacles of government, civil service, law and business. Localisation in all these areas gathered momentum.

This hectic, roller-coaster, politically resigned state of existence was rudely interrupted in the summer of 1989, when the messy but peaceful student demonstrations at the heart of Beijing were violently and bloodily brought to an end by the Chinese Government.

The Tiananmen Square massacre shocked the people of Hong Kong to the core. Overnight they were politicised. In an instant the realities of becoming part of the People's Republic of China were dramatized as if one's worst nightmare was being portrayed in a Hollywood blockbuster. Never have I experienced such an outpouring of genuine public grief and anguish. Millions of Hong Kong people took to the streets in the weeks and months following the massacre to express their distress. It seemed the plans for a smooth handover had been fundamentally derailed.

One effect was a massive boost to the Hong Kong Democrats, fronted by Martin Lee and Emily Lau, in their demands to the British Government to grant Hong Kong people a safe haven, in the form of immigration rights. A second effect was the near breakdown of Sino-British relations as the talks stalled. Another result was the sudden interest of the global community in the Hong Kong issue, as the infamous TV pictures of the tank assault in Beijing flew around the world. But, perhaps the most immediate problem facing the colonial government of the territory was the potential capital flight. For a few precarious weeks, Hong Kong was facing financial meltdown as investors pondered its fate.

Within months British Governor David Wilson, a serious and decent civil servant, announced a plan, cobbled together hurriedly by the Hong Kong business establishment, to restore confidence and prevent financial panic. This centred on building a brand new airport at Chek Lap Kok on the far coast of the island of Lantau. A multi-billion HK Dollar project and engineering tour de force rapidly took shape. This ambitious piece of infrastructural exhibitionism would impress the world and demonstrate the UK's commitment to the people of Hong Kong.

Unfortunately, the People's Republic didn't see it that way and regarded it as a diplomatic slap in the face. They declared their intention to disregard the new airport and even shut it in 1997. In that case it would become a costly great white elephant.

Eventually the British reaction was to replace the low profile foreign office man David Wilson with the flamboyant people's politician Chris Patten. Patten's brief, delivered by the Major government in the UK, was to re-assure the Hong Kong people, and the global audience, that Great Britain was not going to abandon its subjects without a fight... or at least, a strong political gesture. This had become a matter of honour. Late in the historical day as it was, Patten aimed to give Hong Kong a degree of democratic representation that might give them a veneer of self-protection against Beijing when it took over.

A wave of vitriol swept down from the north. The Chinese leaders, labelling Patten "Fat Pang" (he was portly) and a "whore" among other insults, vilified the new governor and the propaganda war quickly became white hot.

Patten, a seasoned popular politician in the UK, once touted leader of the Conservative Party, had purportedly masterminded John Major's surprise electoral victory in 1992. He set about wooing the Hong Kong people with very un-Governor-like behaviour and stacking up votes in Hong Kong's parliament – the Legislative Council – for democratic reform.

He was attacked by Hong Kong's financial elite, both local and colonial, for unnecessarily rocking the boat and stirring up China's wrath. The Foreign Office favoured behind-the-scenes collaboration with China. The Democrats in Hong Kong, on the other hand, demanded full one-man-one-vote representation, and Patten was caught in the crossfire. Consequently, throughout the nineties, in this atmosphere of political hostility, the route to the handover and beyond looked very rocky.

Opinions among the expats varied. Some shared the cynicism of those who thought it nonsense to try to introduce any form of democracy after 150 years of British rule, just a few years before it ended. For others it was a matter of national honour that Britain would depart Hong Kong with some pride that all efforts had been made to give the people a cloak of self-protection in the form of an elected legislature. I placed myself in this camp.

There was little substantive Patten could do except the totemic introduction of some self-rule. However, he and the British Government also set about making sure international attention was fixed on Hong Kong as often as possible so the Chinese government would stick to the Joint Agreement. After much political horse-trading he did manage to introduce elected councillors into the legislature. Hardly one-man, one-vote, but it sent a signal to China that Hong Kong people wanted representation.

Meanwhile, Hong Kong society continued to change at pace. More and more expat, mainly British civil servants, were pensioned off or resigned. Expat policemen were leaving, as were some teachers. Localisation meant they were increasingly replaced by young, educated Hong Kong staff, many of whom had studied in the UK, America, Canada or Australia. In the business world, some expats were also cashing in and trade in Portuguese, Spanish and Australian retirement homes boomed.

For the vast majority of local Hong Kong Chinese, who had neither the skills, nor the capital to secure a second passport overseas, the problem was insurmountable. Some, like my retired schoolteacher friend, Woo Ho Wing, the answer was Singapore. He didn't like that state's paternalistic regime, nor did he care for its stifling equatorial climate, or its regimented spick and span ways. But he emigrated there in the early 90's and stayed for five long, drab years to qualify for Singaporean citizenship. I met him there and over a fish-head curry (the best in Singapore he assured me) he lamented his exile, speaking longingly of the friends, colour and the exuberant untidy energy of Hong Kong, its straight-talking people and overcrowded streets.

As soon as he gained that invaluable passport he returned, but his sacrifice was well worth it, for as a teacher and deeply committed historian, he profoundly mistrusted the Chinese government and remained an admirer of Western democracy.

Another sign of the changing times, as 1997 approached, was the steady scaling down of British forces. It was moving to watch and hear the Black Watch beating the retreat in Happy Valley, as it said farewell to Hong Kong for the last time. It was not so much being impressed by militarism, but witnessing a ceremony that certainly marked the end of an era. It was also a ritual that witnessed the conclusion of a fascinating, and privileged, part of my own life.

The years had passed quickly and it was soon time for the UK, and soon after, for me and my family, to prepare our own farewells. July 1st, 1997, the day of the Handover, after years of negotiation, wrangling, anxiety, doom-saying, vitriol, and patient diplomacy, finally came round. My family and I were firmly in place, as our personal plans in Hong Kong stretched out till at least 2000. I had a moderately successful PR business to run until the turn of the millennium, because of the buy-out arrangement that had come our way. My wife, meanwhile, was finishing off her PhD. We were glad to witness and stay beyond this historic day for Hong Kong, where I had lived for twenty years, where we had met, married and produced a daughter.

Our own plans for this spectacular day of ritual, ceremony and gravity, for that is what the world expected, were determined long before the event. A good friend of ours, journalist Barry and his wife, had with much foresight booked a room at the Excelsior Hotel for the evening and night. He placed the order in 1991, securing the advantage of being on the waterfront, overlooking the harbour. There, we expected to have a panoramic view of the departure of the Royal Yacht Britannia, bearing the last Governor and his family away for the very last time, as well as a magnificent firework display celebrating the assumption of sovereignty by the People's Republic at midnight.

Had Barry been more mercenary, we might never have enjoyed the Excelsior viewing point. Like others, as the day approached, he was offered vast sums, up to $HK7000, to give up the room. But, fortunately for us, history appealed more than filthy lucre! Before we joined our friends at the hotel in the early evening, we watched events unfolding on television. There were many images during that rainy, climactic day, but some stuck out as particularly poignant. There was Patten, with his wife and teenage daughters leaving Government House, not as a stiff shouldered imperial civil servant, but as a family man. They said farewell to a long line of domestic and political staff, both Chinese and expat, with embraces and tears and genuine personal sadness on both sides, obviously magnified by the significance of the occasion.

The Chinese Government had made it quite clear that they would not use the building in any official capacity, so this was a definitive end of era for people and place. Then, later in the afternoon, the formal British farewell ceremony, with key speeches from a lugubrious Prince Charles and a never-say-die Patten, working politician to the end. The event was a dismal affair, with steady, heavy Hong Kong rain pouring down on a sea of umbrellas. In mournful tones the heir to the throne reminded us of the great contribution the UK had made to Hong Kong's development; praised the people of the territory for their entrepreneurship and resilience and promised everlasting support and friendship from the UK.

Patten was more upbeat, talking up the incremental last minute democratic reforms and assuring Hong Kong that it had a great future. He repeatedly pointed out that the eyes of the world were on Hong Kong and its fate would be decided before the moral judgement of a global jury – a not so subtle hint to the Chinese that they needed to honour the agreements over Hong Kong's future. It was a modest comfort to remind ourselves that in Chinese folklore rain means fertility, good crops and therefore prosperity and good fortune. By this measure Hong Kong was set to enjoy bucket loads of good fortune.

A couple of hours later and we were ensconced in our Excelsior viewing room, half-heartedly sipping sparkling wine, watching television for repeats of the day's programme and waiting for the main Handover Ceremony to begin. Our group of four couples were quite subdued. There was neither foreboding nor celebration. Whilst many people suffered from a degree of apprehension, most of us thought Hong Kong was too important for China's modernisation for the new sovereign power to wilfully damage its economic contribution. But there was an underlying suspicion that a one-party ideologically driven government could nevertheless act quite irrationally.

Held in the cavernous Hong Kong Exhibition and Convention Centre, before an audience of over a thousand dignitaries and foreign guests, the main ceremony was dull, contrived and inhibited. Apparently the result of some years of diplomatic wrangling, it was event by committee – uninspiring and cheerless.

Prince Charles represented the Queen. His body language and general tenor betrayed his overall distaste for the formal, militaristic proceedings. Zhiang Zeming, the Chinese Premier, spoke as if he were lecturing a Party Congress in a rather patronising monotone. After a number of speeches, a soldier, sailor and airman of the British forces marched stiffly on to the stage to take down the Union Jack. They were followed by three servicemen of the People's Army, who raised the Chinese Flag.

This military vignette was accompanied by martial trumpet music. It was all rather strained, when it should have been celebratory. It made for compelling TV viewing, but was somehow disappointing, failing to inspire either nostalgia or optimism.

The next act was more emotional, as the TV cameras followed the departing Governor, just before midnight, with his family and entourage down to the Harbour to board the Royal Yacht Britannia and make his final exit of the drama.

It was moving to see them say personal farewells to the many Hong Kong friends and colleagues, who formed long lines leading up to the jetty. At least this was the very human side of the historical happening. Patten was genuinely popular. He had been a refreshing change from his ostrich-feather hatted predecessors, reaching out to the people and coming over as gregarious and sincere. Though many pro-Beijing and business elements hated his democratic reforms, as they upset China, and he was personally vilified, he maintained an approachable and likeable image.

As the rain continued to pour down, as it had all day, the party finally boarded and the yacht pulled away into the gloom of the Harbour. A lingering memory will be of the family waving to friends on the shore and the two Patton daughters shedding a tear and being comforted by their parents. All this we watched in a sombre mood on TV as the view over the harbour from our expensive eyrie was obscured by heavy rain and cloud.

Privately, with a number of selected guests and supporters, the Chinese Government would then, after midnight, celebrate the new sovereign age. A modest firework show would hardly be visible over the rain-drenched harbour.

But the world's cameras, and our attention, was fixed on the border between Hong Kong and China as the minutes and seconds ticked down to midnight. For here the People's Army were mustering, to enter the re-unified territory, long ago lost to the powerful foreigners. Now the tables were turned. However, the situation was sensitive. Any show of tanks or armed might would panic a nervous Hong Kong population, while the world's TV channels would make sure any intimidation would be flashed around the world.

In the event, the images, no less dramatic and symbolic, of PRC's entry, were choreographed to send out a low profile and non-aggressive resumption of power.

There they were, in the teeming rain, pelting down on the roads and drenching them – row after row of straight backed People's Army soldiers in open trucks. No weapons to be seen. No personal carriers. No threats. No noise. Just a silent, almost ghostly column of trucks, waiting at the crossover point. The soldiers, standing to attention, with peaked caps and smart uniforms, all wearing white gloves and gripping the side panel of the open truck. All very disciplined and as unmoving as the terracotta warriors of Xian.

At the stroke of midnight the barriers lifted and the trucks began to roll steadily towards Hong Kong. They would head straight for Victoria Barracks, in central Hong Kong, where they would disgorge their unnerving cargo. No-one in Hong Kong would see or hear a People's Army soldier for many weeks.

We watched mesmerised as this new chapter in Hong Kong's history unfolded. The day had been both moving and anticlimactic. For us expatriates it was the culmination of a time of change, to which we were able to respond with a number of options. For the Chinese residents of Hong Kong, however, it was a new dawn heralding the unknown and the unpredictable, from which they had no escape.

They would be relying on the pragmatism of the Chinese Government; on the moral pressure the international community might bring to bear; but above all on their own remarkable ability to adapt and succeed, to work hard, create and prosper in face of all challenges.

At that moment, and later, wherever fate took me, I earnestly wished Hong Kong to be safe and to continue to thrive.

End